HONDURAS TO HAITI

FIVE YEARS IN THE LIFE OF A SPECIAL FORCES SERGEANT

BY

RONALD W. JOHNSON

24 Sep 06

To my Cousin Billie

Ronald W Johnson

just a little more family history

ISBN: 1-4107-9279-X (e-book)
ISBN: 1-4107-9278-1 (Paperback)

This book is printed on acid free paper.

1stBooks - rev. 02/12/04

DEDICATION

May God forever watch over my daughter and son and
the daughters and sons of the too many good men that I
have known who have died while serving their
country.

At the height of combat operations in Afghanistan very few people are aware there were never more than 300 Special Forces (Green Berets) in that country on any given day. Much has been written of their exploits and their training but nothing has been written about day to day life for these men. Writers or the press are only with them for a few days or weeks at the most, therefore you never get the whole picture of these warriors' lives.

The stories contained in this book are from the authors' personal journals. The book is written as he saw and remembered each event or day and is a record of five years in the life of a senior Special Forces Sergeant as he and his team train, plan and travel around Central and South America and other locations. It is a must for any soldier who might desire to join Special Forces, or has recently become one of the most awesome fighting forces in the world. For the average person or the family member of one of these men it gives one a real look inside of that exciting and dangerous life.

SGM (Retired) David A. (Bear) Martin,
U.S. Army Special Forces

WHY I WROTE THIS BOOK

In the late 70's and early 1980's I was approached on several occasions by young people and asked if I had ever known a particular Sergeant or Captain who had died in Vietnam. When I replied no, I had not served there, a look of disappointment would come over their face. The first few times this occurred I asked why? They would explain that the individual had been their father, that he had been in Special Forces and they were simply hoping that one day they could find a Special Forces soldier who had known them well enough to tell them something about them!

To me this was a terrible way for a young person to go through life. Searching for a stranger who might have known their father. I decide that I would start a journal just in case I also might meet an early demise. I didn't want my children to go through the same turmoil these youth were going through. For that reason this book is dedicated to my children, Nissa and Darius and the many other children of Special Forces soldiers who will never be able to tell their children their story.

There are some gaps in time if you read this book but that's because there was nothing to write about or perhaps in some cases we couldn't write about. I will say this, there is nothing in this book that will disclose classified information nor get a friend shot or divorced. As we say "it's been sanitized to a safe degree"!

RONALD W. JOHNSON

HONDURAS TO HAITI

FROM THE JOURNALS OF

MSG RONALD W. JOHNSON

U.S. ARMY SPECIAL

FORCES

These stories from my personal journals are true; they record five years in the life of a senior Special Forces NCO. It has taken some time to transcribe these events from the chicken scratches in my hand written journals but here they are for others to read. In retrospect, I' m lucky to be alive, some would say, while others would wonder why I haven't been shot, at least once.

January 1989

Here it is, re-enlistment time. What should I do, get out and move the family or re-enlist and remain on active duty? Few might understand this dilemma, but when you grow accustomed to working with the caliber of people found in Special Forces, personal pride makes you want to see if you're as good as the best. There are other reasons. I'm just an old country boy. Nowhere else offers the scope of influence, where what I do can affect the future of so many people and the countries in which they live. When you join Special Forces you become more than a nameless face in an army of a million men; you are one of a very small group. Your efforts and those by your teammates directly affect the success or failure of the mission; this evokes special satisfaction. However, being on the team means always improving because someone is waiting to take your place. Another reason is my desire to develop something to be used by Special Forces, perhaps something on base camps. I've accumulated more information on base camps than anyone else in Special Forces. If I were given the chance to build one, I feel I would then have the credentials to write a book on base camp construction. I have other ideas waiting to be developed.

February 1989

It's Wednesday, the 1st of February; on Friday the 3rd I will leave C/3/5th SFG(A) to be discharged from the Army. I have decided to get out and re-enlist for 7th Special Forces Group (Airborne). Barring unforeseen events, I'll be back in the Army within 30 days. There is an underlying risk, though, since I must retake all the Army entrance exams and the physical. That could prove to be disastrous and could prevent realizing my plans. Oh well, it's worth the risk.

OUT AND IN THE ARMY, AGAIN

On the morning of the 2nd I was sworn back into the Army and received orders for 7th Special Forces Group (Airborne) at Fort Bragg. The family will be happy. I had quite a pleasant surprise on signing the re-enlistment papers. The sergeant informed me that I was entitled a reenlistment bonus because I was an 18F Intelligence Sergeant, who was discharged and was coming back in without being out over three years. What a day! I was also getting paid to come back. At Fort Bragg I stopped by 7th Group Headquarters and told CSM Hank Luthy of the bonus. He cautioned me not to breathe a word to anyone. Should this become public knowledge, there would be a mass exodus and I would be assigned to the 18-series slot with the Eskimo Scouts.

March wasn't all good news. On the 13th a chopper went down in the Arizona desert. On board were members of my old company in 5th Group; everyone perished. Had I not made my decision, it's likely I'd have been with them. Before I left, SGM Billy Hill had told me I would be going to Arizona as intelligence sergeant or the 18F. Additionally the team was a composite team, having been joined ad hoc for the exercise. I knew all 11 on the CH 53; they were from ODAs 591 and 593.

I had known and worked with several of those men for several years. They were CPT Alvin Broussard, a former student; CPT Alan Brown and SFC George Wayne, on the engineer committee at SWCS; and SFC Larry Evans, on the commo committee at SWCS. May God bless all 11 and their families for they were all good men.

7th SPECIAL FORCES GROUP

In 7th Group I was assigned to 1st Battalion. When I reported in CSM Billy Phipps asked me to take over the intelligence/S-2 shop. I said I would consider it and I did. But I really wanted to go to an ODA and be the 18F/intelligence sergeant on the team. I gave him my decision a couple days later and was subsequently assigned to Company A, where the company SGM assigned me to ODA 713. The team sergeant, MSG Ku Chin, welcomed me on board then said that he and the CPT were leaving the next day on the pre-deployment site survey (PDSS) for an exercise in Honduras. I was in charge until their return. They got back and a week later departed on the advance party (ADVON) going down. In the meantime I found that the team had little use for the team leader, CPT Jerry Bailey. Everyone else got along and did his job well. I was still excited to be on the team.

April 1989

HONDURAS, CENTRAL AMERICA

We left Fort Bragg and flew south to Honduras where we landed at Soto Cano Air Base, (SCAB). This was a dusty hellhole built to support operations in Central America and to provide a US presence in country, preventing the Nicaraguans from jumping across the border again. We were lucky; at least we had buildings inside the SF compound in which to sleep and work; many others were sleeping in tents. Everyone except SF was restricted to the base.

ISOLATION

Just before isolation started we were assigned more people to raise team strength to an operation capable level. The additional members brought our total to 11. The team breakdown follows: CPT Jerry Bailey, team leader; CW2 Larry Bush, team tech; MSG Ku Chin, team sergeant; me, intelligence sergeant; SSG Ricky Smith, weapons sergeant; SFC Ross Andrews, senior engineer; SSG Alberto Valerro (RC), junior engineer; SFC Bobby Farris (RC), senior medic; SGT Vinnie Millinger, junior medic; SSG David (Ski) Tomaleski, senior commo; SSG Rob Stewert, junior commo.

On day 2 we went into isolation and learned that we were to hold an unconventional warfare exercise in the Jamastran Valley with 120 Honduran soldiers to be trained as guerillas. On the second day of isolation MSG Chin got sick; the following day he had a family medical emergency back in the States. With all that he was flown out and I took over as team sergeant. I was pretty excited because being team sergeant is something to which all SF NCOs aspire. On the downside I was to keep the CPT on track, not an easy task. It started with the brief back, given by the team to the battalion or group commander, indicating team preparedness. I knew the team needed more rehearsal but he wouldn't hear of it. Infiltration was nearly delayed because of that but we were given the green light.

INFILTRATION

That night we in-filled by two UH-60 Black Hawk helicopters, with half of the team on each bird. Chief Bush and I were in the rear bird. We wore headsets so we could communicate with the aircrew and be informed of we were. We flew into the mountains. I was sitting in the door watching the terrain. The pilot of the front bird was supposed to wear night vision goggles (NVGs); our pilot was only to follow. I was impressed because they were flying lower than usual. Heck, I was looking at the treetops at eye level! Just then our pilot asked the first pilot why he was making so many left and right turns. The following conversation took place:

1. Lead, why are you making all those turns? I thought we were going to fly straight line?
2. What are you talking about, I'm not turning.
1. Yes you are. I'm looking at your boom light and you just made another one.
2. My boom light switch is in the off position.
1. Well it must be stuck on. There, you just turned again.
2. No I didn't. I'll turn my landing light on and you tell me where you are from my position because we're looking around and we don't see you anywhere. There, its on do you see it? (They had my attention now.)

1. I don't see it. Maybe I better turn mine on. #!/*
   (as we pulled up) I've been following a!*# pick-up
   truck with no headlights and only one taillight.

   With that our pilot found the other bird and we
proceeded south. I glanced at my watch and realized
we were coming upon the town of Danli, where we
would turn NE toward the Jamastran Valley. I looked
down and saw the "Y" in the road with the statue in the
center. I figured the pilots would turn on the south
side but they kept on flying. The lead pilot told ours
we would turn at the next town. I felt it was time to
speak up. "Hey sir, this is the team sergeant. That last
town was Danli and we should have turned there."
"No, this next town is Danli." "No sir. I saw the "Y"
with the statue in it. The next town is El Perrisio and
we don't want to get over it. We do and we will be in
range of those SA-14s from Nicaragua." Chief Bush
broke in and told the pilot I was right. Our pilot shared
this with the lead, who quickly turned, saying we
would fly back, find the "Y" and get back on route.
These two pilots weren't from Task Force 160, the
Special Ops Aviation unit, and I doubt they ever made
it. They even had trouble finding our landing zone
(LZ). We finally picked a spot and told them to just let
us off, which they did.

MOVEMENT TO LINK-UP
We somehow found the other half of the team
and moved on, the CPT in front and me in the rear. An
hour later, while crossing a dirt road/danger zone, we
came to a sudden stop. With the two men in front of
me, I moved to the side of the road, not knowing why

we had stopped. After a bit I went up front to find out. What I discovered was that the CPT had simply decided to stop where he was and call in the Initial Infil Report. I commented on the poor location, suggesting that we go deeper into the woods. With great annoyance he said he was making the commo shot and the team was not to move until he finished. Mad as hell, I returned to the rear. While lying there I heard a sound that sent shivers up my spine: a plastic rifle stock that slapped against something metal.

The noise came from up the road; then I heard voices. We were in an area the Nicaraguans had invaded the year before, one through which terrorists and Contras moved regularly. And lastly there was a Honduran battalion in the area; goodness only knew how many civilians were armed. And there we were, sitting ducks in a ditch beside the road. I didn't dare move much but I did slide my hand down to undo the flap on my holster. All of us had live ammo in our pistols. No one moved as three Hondurans went by, less than 25 feet away. I could see they had an M-16 and two FN-FAL rifles. One rode a bicycle. After walking another 25 or 30 yards, they turned up a driveway to a house about 50 yards off the road. A dog at the house then started barking; I didn't think he would ever stop. I continued to lie in the ditch, watching one of the Hondurans walk around the perimeter of the yard; he passed within 15 feet and as he did so I saw he was armed. Thanks to the weeds he couldn't see us. At last we started moving again.

I noticed as we walked that each time we came to a fence, instead of climbing over or under it, the fence got cut. These weren't shoddy fences; they were first rate, six-strand fences. I sent word up to cease cutting fences. Five minutes later I heard another wire being cut. I advanced to the front, where the CPT was cutting another wire. I asked CPT Thomas, our evaluator, and Chief Bush to come up to where we were. I advised the CPT not to cut another fence. He replied that he would cut as many fences as he wished.

Having reached my limit of tolerance, I informed him that if he cut another fence he would be relieved for willfully destroying private property, recklessly endangering his men, and attempting to create an international incident. I then informed CPT Thomas for the record that the CPT had been warned. While I walked off, I heard Chief Bush say that that he hated to go against the CPT but I was right. In Texas people were shot for what the CPT was doing. I sincerely hoped he would not cut any more fences. It must have worked; no more were cut. The CPT violated more rules of movement that night than anyone I had ever witnessed. As we continued to move toward the linkup point he straight lined our route, even passing in front of a small bar. Luckily no one came outside. Then came a near shoot out.

THE LUMBER YARD

On our approach to a lumberyard I knew our route would take us through the main building. I wondered if the CPT would go through the back door and out the front. Although he didn't, the point man was not directed to go around the danger area. SSG Smith, who was pulling point, was moving past the corner of the office when a guard appeared, armed with a FN-FAL and accompanied by a German Shepherd. They stood face to face, each with his rifle pointed at the other, Smith with blanks and the guard with a twenty-round magazine in a fully automatic weapon. That guard had to be terrified. Before him stood 10 soldiers, camouflaged and armed with M-16 rifles. His fear could be heard in his voice. Heck, who wouldn't have been scared? I realized this was the worst situation possible. Here was a guy with every right in the world to fire, while all we could do was pray he wouldn't. I was the only one who could move into position where, if he fired, I could return fire. I moved to my left, taking cover behind a dirt pile and dropping my ruck. I then removed the blank adapter and loaded live ammunition. To save the lives of my men, I had no choice but to shoot the guard if he were to fire.

I positioned myself at the top of the dirt pile, keeping my sights on the guard. I prayed that all of us, the guard included, would get out safely. Chief Bush and CPT Thomas, both of whom spoke excellent Spanish, moved forward. After five or six minutes Chief ordered the men to move out while he, CPT Thomas and CPT Bailey continued to talk. I quickly moved back in line and walked backwards to keep an eye on the situation. After a bit the other three said good-bye and started our way.

While we moved from there, I walked immediately behind the point man. When we finally took a break the CPT tried to retake the front position. I politely declined, telling him that twice that night he had almost caused men to be shot. The only way he would lead was if he relieved me as team sergeant. I continued to lead and that morning we linked up with the Honduran unit that was to play the part of our guerilla unit.

The next day, the company commander, MAJ Ed Phillips, took the CPT to the woods. When he came back he declared that the CPT would henceforth pay attention or else. He also asked that I keep the CPT out of trouble. Hey, what's a team sergeant for?

THE ARTEP

There were 120 Hondurans to train during our ARTEP. We tried to make the training the best we could. The unit had just finished basic training and we would be their Advance Individual Training (AIT). Thirty days afterward they would deploy along the Nicaraguan boarder. On those rotations three to four men would usually be lost to land mines; that's why we worked hard. The Jamastran Valley, during April and most of May, is dry. While moving around the valley it was not uncommon for us to push and shove horses or cattle out of a spring or water trough in order to share their water. I don't remember how far it is around that valley but we walked every foot of it.

Because we lacked cover and concealment, it was impossible to keep the entire group together.

What we did was break down into smaller groups to avoid detection then join for specific operations. This strategy worked well. When Chief and I left our group that last morning, we began to walk to the linkup point several miles away. We walked and we walked. About 1600 hours we arrived at a small shop that sold Cokes and fruit. Chief and I hadn't had a Coke in almost three weeks. We stopped, drank three apiece, then bought a watermelon and ate it. I still remember how hard it was to resume walking.

That night, when time came to exfiltrate, we were to be picked up by helicopter. Although we were at the right place at the right time, no chopper came. All of us were exhausted and had eaten the last of our food that morning. To make matters worse, it was raining cats and dogs and the night had turned cold. Finally we got radio notification that no chopper could fly over the mountains that night. I gathered the men and we looked for shelter. About a mile away was a barn that belonged to a Honduran general's brother. The general and US DEA agents had arrested him the year before, so we figured no one would mind us using the barn. That's where we stayed until the next night, when we again waited several hours for choppers to arrive. Of course it was raining again; the rainy season had arrived. The choppers never came but a couple of trucks did; we chose to leave on those. On the drive back, while coming around a turn, we saw what resembled a log in the road. We swerved to avoid it. As we continued I shouted for the driver to stop. What we had thought was a log was really one very large snake. We ran back to check the snake out but it had crawled away.

A FRIEND IS LOST

We did receive some devastating news in the midst of everything going well. We got word that COL James (Nick) Rowe had been murdered by a Philippino communist hit team, known as a Sparrow team. Using several automatic weapons, they had attacked COL Rowe in his armored automobile. One bullet made it through a crack between the door and door post and struck him. He was one of the best known and best liked officers in recent Special Forces. He had been my battalion commander. I have signed copies of the first photos taken after his escape from five years as a POW in Vietnam. I also have a signed copy of his book, "Five Years to Freedom." I considered him a friend. We had discussed my going to the Philippines with him. When I declined, believing I could do more with 7th Group, he was quick to say I should go to 7th Group. He also felt he would not come home this time, knowing that the communists had long memories and had lost face when he escaped. He was certain this time he would not escape.

May 1989

BACK AT SOTO CANO AIR BASE (SCAB)

We spent several days at Soto Cano, resting and repacking, preparing to conduct a combat lifesaver course and light infantry course for the 9th Battalion. CPT Baily, SSG Smith, and a new team member, SFC Tim Wynne, went down a couple of days before our departure date to begin construction at our campsite.

Early on the day we were to return, it began to rain. It was dark and still raining when we arrived. Our campsite was at the other end of the battalion area, across a creek. The creek had risen somewhat, so I wondered if it was safe to cross. Chief and Ski insisted it was. Both had been here the year before and swore that the creek was only two feet at its deepest. Someone on the other side was waving us on, so I decided to give try. We were driving a Dodge 4 x 4 with plenty of weight on it. The other bank had almost no slope at all. I put the truck in low four-wheel drive. Chief and another member was up front with me; two or three guys were in the back of the truck with the equipment. I warned everyone to hold tight in case things got rough. As I started forward I said to Chief, "I sure hope you guys are right." It was then that the front wheels suddenly dropped about six inches, but I couldn't stop now. Almost as quickly the lights went under water and it was dark. Chief was saying, "Don't stop now!" I glanced at him to reply but saw water about three inches up against the side window. The truck was in second gear and low drive, so I gave it a little more gas. Meanwhile Ski and the others were climbing on top of the equipment. We were still moving. The defroster then started blowing water up on the inside of the windshield. We continued to move in a straight line, though. The front of the truck then began to climb up the other side. Next the headlights reappeared. With that we continued up and out of the creek. Everyone was cheering and laughing. I climbed out and shouted to the others on the other side to pull their truck back up the road and sleep in it. No one else was to try crossing until morning.

Our cheers turned to disbelief: in front of the truck our equipment, which had come only two days before, floated in a small lake. And there stood CPT Bailey in the door of his tent, clad in his underwear, scratching his privates. The others and I were furious. We grabbed the equipment and moved it into a tent or placed it up on something and covered it. A short while later I sat on a cot, salvaging what I could from my food box, steam rising from me. Ski was just as mad. He threw something out the door and sat back down I lifted my mess kit out of the box, remarking that "at least the water didn't screw up everything;" I poured a pint of water from the mess kit onto the floor. Ski and I looked at each other and started laughing. We were simply too disgusted. We had battled against stupidity, ignorance and laziness far too many days and for a while no longer cared. Once again we were wet, tired, hungry, and totally screwed, a condition that was becoming the norm.

SUCCESS ON SUCCESS

The next day was considerably improved. The creek was down, the sun was out and we could finish most of the camp while our gear dried. Yet, despite all the mishaps mentioned to this point, there were also many successes. As a team we were beginning to look good and to perform well. Even the CPT was starting to listen to those who tried to help him.

THE COMBAT LIFESAVER COURSE

This phase of the deployment began with the Combat Lifesaver Medical Course, which lasted about

2½ weeks. The training went well as everyone was involved in different phases. The final exercise was the course highlight. There were different stations to where students were to carry a patient-bearing litter. At each station a different medical task was to be performed. The last station was the best. We had dug a hole into which the role player, his legs bent at the knee, could place the lower half of his legs. We then cut a pair of pants up the back to insert mannequin legs, which would appear lifelike. One leg was then turned at an odd angle, seemingly broken. The other would be doused with lighter fluid and the lower half lit as the worn students climbed over the bank. How I wish I could have captured some of those students' faces on camera. The victim would lie on the ground, one leg appearing to be broken, the other on fire, screaming as if he were in real pain. A few times he would see the expression on one of his friend's face, and would break out in laughter. At times we, too, broke out in laughter. The students were to run and with an old blanket on the ground smother the fire and assess the injuries. Oh yes, the victim had a simulated wound on his stomach and another on his head. He looked like hell.

WHERE ARE WE, AL?

Other accomplishments were occurring at the same time. We were assisting the battalion assembling target folders for all the bridges in their area. All the dimensions were marked on the photos, where to place the charges and how much. One day SSG Al Valerro and I went to photograph a bridge; I drove and he read the map. My team was the only one allowed within

10K of the boarder and the bridge we planned to photograph wasn't too far north of it. I would ask Al if he could find this or that landmark on the map; he would reply, "Yeah, we're OK." After a while I became a little concerned; by now we should be quite close. I asked Al what I should find on taking the next turn. Suddenly Al wasn't so sure where we were. At last we reached a bridge so I pulled over to look at the map. Without being certain, I felt we were almost at the boarder. Then came an old man with his burro. I had Al ask the man where we were. If the old man didn't know, Al was to ask for directions to Chi Chi Caste, a small town I believed to be north of our present location. I had just finished taking photos when Al walked back. He informed me that Chi Chi Caste was to the left and straight ahead was a Nicaraguan border checkpoint, at the top of the hill about 800 meters from us. We took our measurements on key components and immediately boarded the truck and drove north.

THE ANTI PERSONNEL MINE

Collecting intelligence information was another task in which we excelled. The Hondurans had brought us an antipersonnel mine for identification. We researched all our available books but couldn't determine the type. So we photographed the mine then sent it to J-2 at SCAB. The following day the mine came back. It seems someone had shown it to the LTC, who wondered if it was live and someone said he thought so. Apparently the LTC then screamed out an order to remove the mine. As no one knew what else to do with it, the mine was brought back. It was a live mine but was not armed or fixed with a detonating cap. In other words, NO WAY could it blow!

It being a Saturday, we set up some targets around the mine and with our video camera filmed the mine as it detonated. We filmed the results as well. Two hours later a LTC and a MAJ from MILGRP arrived, wondering if we still had the mine. We all looked at each other and went, oops! We explained that we had just blown the mine up earlier that day. They seemed disappointed so we told them about the film and photographs, which of course they wanted to see. We played the tape and afterward they wanted both tape and photos. I asked how badly they wanted a mine since we had proven it had been manufactured in the 50s. They were enthusiastic in their wish to have one, so I told them to grab a Coke from the cooler and to have a seat. Next I called SSG Valerro and told him to find another mine. I walked over to Al and quietly told him to get the one in the ammo bunker. The LTC and MAJ did not hear me. I also told him to take his time returning as I wanted the extra time to talk with them about what we had been doing. I knew they would talk to others when they got back. A little PSYOPs goes a long way. He returned about 25 minutes later, to their pleasure.

THE TERRORIST CAMPS

Chief and I had an excellent intelligence source, who told us the location of two terrorist camps less than 10K south of the boarder. We reported the information, which of course was questioned. We provided the general grid location and challenged them to do an over flight for verification. I knew this was happening because Nicaragua had been moving troops up to within 10-20K of the boarder. Quite a few troops, to be exact, and everyone knew it. They did the over flight and came back to us, astounded by the accuracy of our report. After that our reports were never again questioned we were encouraged to continue. It wasn't long before we were reporting enemy positions and large movements, all thanks to our source.

A SICK WOMAN

A young man from Nicaragua was brought to us by guards one day. On hearing that nearby were Americans who had a doctor, he had risked capture and had walked out of his country. We had no doctor but did have our medics, as good as or better than any doctor to be found in such a remote area. He had come to seek help for his ailing mother, whom he thought to be dying. He asked that we go to his village to help her. That this was a possible trap had to be considered, as was the impossibility of our crossing the boarder. The CPT, Chief and I together formulated a viable plan. We agreed to examine the boy's mother but she had to come to us. At best, our helping her would ensure that the family would spread the word. At worst, they would know that we tried. Our plan with its PSYOP value was presented to the Honduran battalion commander, who enthusiastically accepted it. His S-2 was to propose a site where the boy and his mother were to cross the boarder. A company of soldiers was to be in place to prohibit enemy soldiers crossing at that point after them. His bringing the boy and his mother to us 10K on this side would also make it difficult for the enemy to reach us. That next day the young man was briefed on what to do, as well as when and where to cross.

A few days later the boy and his mother crossed the boarder without incident. When they reached camp SGT Millinger and SFC Farris examined the woman, took samples, and began the tests. She was found to be suffering from a parasitic infection. Millinger and Farris consulted the doctors at SCAB, who confirmed the infection and recommended antibiotics. These antibiotics were available on site so SGT Millinger initiated treatment. Soon after the patient was sufficiently well to return home. She was provided enough medications to complete her course. Both were also educated on the most likely cause and preventing recurrence. The Hondurans then arranged for their safe passage back across the border. Another successful joint operation could be reported.

A SHOT IN THE DARK
One morning, about 3 o'clock, a guard assigned to our camp perimeter heard a noise in the brush. We heard him call out "Alto!"(stop). Several of us were immediately wide awake. When the guard fired a shot, we moved from our bunks to pre-assigned locations, our weapons ready. We all heard someone or something running away. The next morning we searched the general area and found tracks but no blood trail. To reward his alertness, the guard was given a Meal Ready to Eat (MRE), quite significant in

a unit where two-three small meals daily were all to be had.

That next night there was, we thought, a repeat performance. About 1 a.m. another guard was heard to call out "Alto!" At the same time we heard him flip the safety off his M-16. But this time to the challenge there was a reply from his first sergeant. The guard seemed disappointed; I think he wanted a free meal too. But after a minute or two he seemed convinced the intruder really was his first sergeant.

A PSYCHO FROG

In a situation like ours silly things were often done for entertainment. One of the nightly occurrences was the appearance of giant, 2-pound frog who came around 7 p.m. For amusement we took turns knocking a large beetle off the tent wall, picking up the beetle and dropping it a few inches in front of the frog. We would then watch the frog pop the beetle with its long tongue. We then wondered how many he could eat before he was full; his record, I think, was 23 beetles in one night. He was jokingly called Smitty.

About 3 o'clock one morning he hopped into the tent. My bunk was halfway down one side of the tent and there was where he stopped. Soon everyone was shouting at me to do something about Smitty. He was croaking what sounded like "feed me;" at least everyone agreed that was what it sounded like. Tired of the ragging I was getting, I finally picked him up and took him outside; five minutes later he was back. What was wrong with this psycho frog? This time I took him outside to the side of the creek and pitched him in the water; that was that for the night. The next night when he showed up at his customary time, I dropped a beetle in front of him. He hopped up into the air and turned around, declining the free meal. After that he never again accepted another beetle from me, from anyone else he would but not from me. His nightly appearances continued until our departure. Smitty was one strange frog. If I didn't have witnesses to this I sure wouldn't speak of it.

THE FIRST JOINT HONDURAN AND CONTRA OPERATION

The Hondurans told us of a reported crossing by a Nicaraguan terrorist unit at the boarder between our site and Danli. They requested assistance in planning an operation to find the Nicaraguans. We went to Battalion HQs to do so. I thought of contacting the contras near Danli; one of them might know of possible routes the terrorists could use. Also they might have trackers. The contras were quite happy to assist those who were providing them a country in which to live. We notified US MILGRP of the operation but whoever Chief spoke with did not believe the operation was going on, declaring instead that notification would have been given by the Honduran command. Chief was not given the chance to say we had helped plan it before the guy hung up. A couple of days later we got a call from someone at MILGRP. How, he wondered, did we know of the operation at the same time it was being launched? Our reply, of course, was that we had helped in the plans. Why didn't we say so before, he asked. I told him the guy we spoke with before said we didn't know what we were talking about and hung up on us to quickly. Surely someone back there got his tail chewed out over that.

CHANGE OF COMMAND

While we were with them the Honduran battalion had a change of command. That day the Honduran chief of staff came with his bodyguard detail. They looked impressive, one more so than the others; we all noted this. After the ceremony the general asked to meet the Green Beret team, who had stood in rank with the Hondurans during the ceremony. The CPT came down the rank and introduced each of us. Suddenly I was tackled by the security guard we had all noticed. He was saying, "SGT Johnson! SGT Johnson!" I got a good look. It was CPT Geraldo Wildt Morales, a former student of mine during Phase III at the Special Warfare Center and School. It was great to see him and we were able to continue our friendship.

AN INSTANT MEETING CLOSURE

Our daily team meeting, during which we discussed the next day's training, was usually held under a large fig tree. I was concluding the meeting when the guy on the end of the table, who had been leaning way back, suddenly doubled forward and fell out of his chair. A large baseball sized fig had apparently fallen from the tree and had landed on his family jewels. The meeting thus ended as we helped him to his bunk.

A WEEKEND WHERE!

The medical training was finished and a weekend off was long overdue. But there was a slight problem. Most of the team wanted to go to Tegucigalpa, (Tegu) the capital city, about 120K away. So getting there was difficult. Also, the Maya, which was the main hotel, was expensive and usually full. We went to Tegu anyway. I called Geraldo and asked if he knew of a place, relatively secure, where we could wind down. He thought he knew of a suitable place. When we linked up with him, he took us on the road to the Valley of the Angels. About halfway there we pulled into a love motel. This was a motel where a man and his girlfriend or mistress could drive through the gate into the garage and from there go straight to the room. The rooms rented for two to four hours. Geraldo spoke with the owner and got us rooms for $12 per night. She told us we were the first to stay who required daily rates and had no accompanying women. This place had everything we needed: a 12-foot surrounding wall, armed security, and nearby restaurants. The hotel was fairly new, very clean, had large beds and privacy, and best of all, large showers with plenty of hot water. On Saturday we drove to the Valley of the Angels and bought gifts to take home. Because it was the artisan center for the country, it was an ideal place to shop. Leather and wood items, paintings, carvings and many other items were available. We also went downtown to eat. Before we could leave on Sunday, the owner insisted on having a cookout for us. We were also the first Americans to stay there she said.

LIGHT INFANTRY TRAINING

On our return from Tegu, another company was ready to begin three weeks of light infantry training. We were off and running again. Training included marksmanship, land navigation, the whole nine yards. Everything went well. Last was a live fire exercise, where the students would demonstrate all they had learned. We opened with 106-mm recoilless rifles and 50-caliber machineguns; the students fired their rifles. As the students moved forward the 106s and 50s shifted fire to the right. For added realism, as the students moved forward, we had quarter-pound TNT charges detonating in front of them. At the same time many other things happened in the last three weeks.

June 1989

AN EMERGENCY OPERATION

SGT Millinger sometimes drank excessively, so I had cut his drinking off. I counseled him, telling him that sobriety was necessary in his role as medic. He could one day find himself operating on someone he knew. Not only would he know the patient but the wife and children too. If he performed badly, he would have to face the man's family. Two weeks later that exact situation occurred. He said later that those were his exact thoughts just before he made the first cut.

HOTEL EVACUATION

The Friday following our weekend in Tegu, Chief, a couple of the other guys and I were going to Danli to eat. Halfway there a car pulled up behind us, its lights blinking on and off. Thinking this could be the enemy, we readied our pistols. It was our source.

He reported that his most trusted man on the other side of the border had sent word that terrorists were planning to kidnap an American at the Maya hotel that weekend. He suggested that we call someone. We returned to camp; this was a hot one! We had to decide whom to call and what to say. We felt the message should be high priority, but how high to make it? There was much to consider. Unclear wording or too low in urgency, and nothing would be done. Too high and anything could result. Chief and I had a tough call to make. To this time our source had been completely dependable. We finally gave the message the highest rating possible.

In doing so the Ambassador was forced to order evacuation of all Americans from the Maya that night. Had we been wrong, we would have been accountable to many high-ranking people. On Saturday the Hondurans caught three of five terrorists waiting outside the Maya to kidnap an American. This was crucial for reasons other than safety of Americans. The following week Vice-President Dan Quayle was to be in town. The terrorists had hoped to succeed, thus causing Mr. Quayle to cancel his trip and resulting in loss of face for the US.

DEAD-EYE SMITTY
The Sunday afternoon after the hotel evacuation SSG Smith, SFC Farris and I were the only ones in camp, the others having gone to town to eat. I

told Ricky and Bobby to burn out the latrine. This is a barrel, cut in half, then placed in a shallow hole in the ground and a seat placed on top and used as a latrine. They went to the field to burn it out and returned within 20 minutes. Ricky explained that even after diesel fuel had been added, there was too much waste liquid in the latrine barrel for it to burn. I instructed them to cover the top of the barrel with target cloth then to fire a few rounds from the 9-mm pistol through the cloth to knock holes in the bottom. I also reminded them to notify the guards that they were going to fire. Shortly thereafter, I heard a shot then a scream. I thought someone had been shot so I ran toward them. I met Ricky on the way so I asked him what had happened. He didn't reply but kept going. Before I could get angry, I smelled something foul. I knew then what had happened. Ricky had fired down into the barrel without first covering the top. He suffered the consequences of disobeying orders with a self inflicted covering of waste content from the barrel. I continued up the trail and found Bobby on the ground, holding his sides and laughing hysterically, tears pouring down his face. After both of us stopped laughing he and I returned to camp and found Ricky, bathing in the creek and washing a uniform.

WATER BOMB AWAY

Up the road about 60K was another team from 7th Grp. Fact is, this was the team whose member had undergone an appendectomy by SGT Millinger. Their water was being flown in by helicopter in blivets with 2000-pound water capacity. A young Honduran soldier was washing his captains Toyota pickup truck

He waved to the pilot, who mistakenly thought the soldier wanted the blivet loaded into the pickup truck. The young soldier was frantically waving him away when the blivet was released. That blivet landed in the back of the truck and broke the truck in half. Needless to say the US bought a pickup truck that day. I think a helicopter crew paid Uncle Sam later.

AFTER DINNER EXCITEMENT

Just before we left the valley, CPT Bailey, SSG Stewart and I went to Danli for dinner. We picked a restaurant in which we had previously eaten several times before. After dinner, we were drinking a beer when two guys came in. We judged by the way they looked our way several times that they wanted something. Before we could finish and leave they came over and started a discussion with us. They were hardcore communists who were trying to draw us into an altercation. The situation was turning ugly so I excused myself to go to the restroom. While there I took out my pistol, chambered a round, and stuck the pistol in my belt. I then went back outside and sat down in a different spot from where I could watch the bad guys. A short time later the owner ordered the two to leave. Had they been from Danli, they would not have started trouble in a restaurant owned and run by Contras. We decided to stay another 30 minutes and to allow those two time to get far away. We weren't looking for any trouble.

Outside we looked around and decided it was OK to go. I had just backed the van out and was leaving the parking lot when these two blocked the exit with their car then jumped out with assault rifles, AK-47s. We rolled out of the van with our pistols; that is, two of us did. The CPT had left his pistol at the camp. He said, "Top, give me your pistol!" I told him to be prepared to run when the shooting started. Rob had his pistol and each of us had a man in his sights. I covered the one on my left and Rob had the one on the right. We held our fire, wanting to shoot only as a last resort. If they didn't point their rifles at us, we wouldn't fire.

They wanted us to follow them down the road. Right! We were brain-dead. They were getting agitated and making me nervous when from our right we heard someone telling them to leave now or they wouldn't be leaving at all. I looked in that direction and saw four men from the restaurant armed with FN-FAL rifles. I grinned at the fact that the odds were now in our favor. Realizing the need to leave, the bad guys did just that. We returned to camp after reporting the incident to the police. Oh, yeah, the area commander for the police was a little annoyed that we had not shot the bad guys. We explained that we wanted to avoid an international incident so did not wish to shoot them unless it became necessary. If it happened again, he said, we were to go ahead and shoot. He would make sure two of his men were credited for the shooting and no one would ever know. We thanked him, saying we would keep that in mind.

WINDUP TO A GOOD TRIP

During the 1st Battalion commander's out brief to the Honduran chiefs of staff ours was the only ODA mentioned by team number for our consistently outstanding performance. What a great way to finish the trip! The team had finally come together and had worked hard to overcome many problems.

Above: SSG Millinger observes 9th Bn students during medical training testing.
Below: Another student during medical testing.

Me standing with the Honduran officers during the graduation ceremony. SSG Rob Stewart and SSG Ross Andrews sitting.

Below: Inside the Special Forces compound at Soto Cano Air Force Base (SCAB) in 1989. View is from a team room hooch with the headquarters on the left and a mortor bunker on the far right.

July 1989

ITS NOW MINE TO KEEP

Back at Fort Bragg some business had to be taken care of before we could take leave. After that and before I went on leave, the company commander informed me that I would keep the team. MSG Chin would not be returning.

October 1989

DEPLOYMENT TO PANAMA

After an unsuccessful coup attempt by some of the members of the Panama Defense Force officers, we deployed to Panama as part of a security enhancement program. The political and criminal situation in Panama had worsened to the point that it had become necessary to help protect US interest and US civilians and dependents. While there we were to conduct team training as well as security or combat operations if the situation continued to deteriorate. My team also served as B-team support. I was team sergeant and acting company S4. B-team support can be one big headache but each team rotated; it was our turn. A supply MOS was fortuitously in my background.

We left Fort Bragg with plenty of ammunition for training but almost had to return some of it before we left. It seemed that our being given all the 9-mm ammo we had requested resulted in none left for 7th Group FY 1st quarter. The Group asked us to transfer the ammo over to 2nd Battalion but regulation prohibited that practice, something I had to prove as high as the group commander. Several of the group staff thought they knew regulations better than I did and said so to the Group Commander. The controversy was resolved when Group received a letter from the post ammunition supply point The letter, sent at my request, even declared that the ammunition could be lost for use or someone could be charged. We therefore took the ammunition south but not without another good story.

WHERE ARE THE BLASTING CAPS?

We loaded equipment, ammunition and demolitions on the airplane. I had been working nonstop and had gone two days without sleep. The last item loaded was the case of blasting caps to be used for the demolitions. I watched as the case was tied down on the ramp by the aircraft crew chief and I watched as both ends of that C5 were closed. At last there was nothing more to do. I climbed the stairs to the passenger section but rather than sitting in a seat, I lay on the floor on my poncho liner. I remembered nothing else until we landed in Panama.

The jolt of the wheels touching the runway at Howard AFB awoke me. After shaking the last of the sleep off, I retrieved my gear and went to the cargo area ahead of everyone else. I have always been fastidious about blasting caps because the rules for handling them are very strict. I was totally confused; there were no caps to be found. An entire 1000-count case of caps was gone! The tie-down straps remained but no caps. I mentally reviewed everything, certain that I had loaded the caps. SGM Stone walked up grinning and asked, "Where are your caps?" The look on my face was reportedly indescribable because all I could reply was that the caps had disappeared!!! Stone said they were still at Fort Bragg. That's not possible, I protested, I had seen the case loaded and tied down, and the doors to the plane closed before I came upstairs. By SGM Stone's report, back at Fort Bragg with the plane taxiing, the pilot inquired about explosives on board. He became very excitable when he realized that under him was a case of blasting caps. He immediately stopped the plane and had the caps unloaded. My stomach did a flip-flop. Now I was sick. I demanded to know why no one had awakened me. I shouted that the stupid #@!!*?+#!@ pilot didn't know his own regulations; we were perfectly correct, by regulations. Stoney said then that several people tried to wake me but the moment I laid down I was OUT. They tried for 10 minutes, without success. By this time I was really worried about the caps. "I'm the one who signed for them and now I don't know where they are!" Stoney calmly explained that the battalion commander, LTC Jones, was there when the plane stopped and the caps put out on the runway. LTC Jones drove out on the runway to find out why. That horse's rear air-taxi driver still adamantly refused to have the caps on the plane. How, I wondered, did he become a colonel in the Air Force? LTC Jones took the caps back to the unit in his military vehicle and somehow managed to bring them a few weeks later, when he arrived with some men from our MI detachment.

ARRIVAL IN PANAMA

Soon after the equipment was unloaded, our Panama Defense Force (PDF) escort arrived and together, in convoy, we headed for Fort Sherman on the other side. I climbed into the front of a truck and went to sleep. At Fort Sherman we joined our ADVON party.

SGT Sanders, company supply sergeant, was excited about the ammo left behind by C/2/7 for which he had signed. He gave me the 5515R, a legally worthless document; I quoted him the regulation. At the bunker I kept our ammo separate from that left behind, at least until the legal issue had been resolved.

We stayed in Battery Pratt, a WW II gun battery 40 feet underground. It was fairly large, with steel doors in the front and the rear. Except for chow it had everything needed to accommodate an entire SF company. It was cool at night so we slept in sleeping bags and during the day was comfortable inside. We would emerge at times to conduct training and return there.

To complicate the ammunition issue, the departing unit had failed to clear its ammunition documents prior to leaving the country. A few days later we were told by group to clear the other unit's documents (DA 581s), which was impossible because of the questionable procedures followed by the other company (giving ammo to any unit that wanted it, without benefit of accompanying paperwork). I asked the company commander, MAJ Perez, to notify Group of this.

Around 0430 one morning we got alerted for a threat situation, a contingency for which I had planned. Six of us immediately went to the ammo storage point four miles away. Within 27 minutes of being awakened I was back, issuing ammunition to the company. We set a speed record that morning for that road. Whether the exercise was practice or real we never found out. We stood down about 0600 hours.

November 1989

Back to the ammo situation. Group did not believe how complicated the situation had become so the deputy commander (DCO), LTC DeJesus came for an evaluation, although I personally believe it was to tear-up my backside. I was the one who had discussed the issue with the ammunition surveillance people at Fort Davis and simply would not allow my commander's career ruined for someone else. It was late when LTC DeJesus arrived, around 9:00 p.m. After I had told him what I knew, he was understandably furious, but not at us. He called Fort Bragg and demanded that 2nd Battalion send someone, a MAJ or above, immediately and that someone better have the clear/readable DA 581s in hand. He also called the Group finance officer and ordered him to be prepared to cut travel orders that night. I offered my assistance recovering and clearing the problem; more than 15,000 rounds had come back with even more coming.

A NEW SNIPER RIFLE

Around this time the new M-24 sniper rifles were issued. I took mine to my sleeping area for disassembling and cleaning. After trying the trigger a few times, I thought I could improve it. I stoned the parts for smoother function then reassembled the rifle. In doing so, a half-moon clip flew off. With some 20 minutes of crawling around on the floor I found it. The next day at the rifle range we were starting the zero process for the system when one of the other teams showed up. SFC Makar asked to shoot mine.

While he was shouldering the rifle, I told him just how light the trigger was. He lowered the barrel to take aim, removed the safety, and placed his finger on the trigger. Bam! He agreed that the trigger was indeed light. Chief and I liked our rifles; we could do some serious shooting with these.

One of the team sergeants, MSG Jeff Graham, was leaving so we had a toga party in the Bat Cave (what everyone called Battery Pratt). As parties go, this was a good one. Jeff got plastered and at one point was carried on a litter. I doubt he could have walked anyway.

SCRATCH TWO FRIENDLIES

One training night we were conducting an assault on Battery McKenzie. Several teams opened up with rifle and machinegun fire. SFC Makar and his team came in by helicopter. We ceased fire as they fast-roped on top of the battery. We then rushed in to assist clearing the many rooms. Fortunately we were using blanks. In the last room SFC Makar and his team threw in some grenade simulators. Boom! Boom! Then they rushed inside, firing as they did so. SFC Makar shouted cease-fire. Under a cot and a table were two young Marine privates, almost in shock. They were shaking, couldn't hear, and could hardly speak. While the medics were treating the Marines, MAJ Perez called post operations by radio. He had operations contact the Marine OIC because they had been told to stay away from that area, yet there they were, with two soldiers injured. The Post Commander, LTC Richards was quite disturbed. They never came that way afterward. Had they been there the night before they might have been killed; that one was a live fire on the site.

December 1989

RICK GOES FOR A SWIM

On weekends we often swam and snorkeled either at Hidden Beach, next to Fort San Lorenzo (an old Spanish Fort) or just outside the front gate of Fort Sherman. We would also go to Shimmy Beach on Fort Sherman to play volleyball and to swim. One of the guys, SFC Rick Lazares asked me to swim out to a boat with him. When I asked which boat, he pointed to one large green Toyota car hauler about 5000 meters out. I told Rick he was out of his mind. We'd been drinking and the distance was too long without fins. After begging me to go and my declining, he swam off by himself. When he had gone 200 meters or so the lifeguard warned me that if my friend didn't come back he would call the MPs. To avoid trouble, I got my fins out and swam out after Rick. He wasn't wearing fins so I was able to catch him. Rick thought I had decided to join him but I told him why I had come after him. He gave me a message for the lifeguard: to kiss his rear. I won't put what he actually said. He continued on his way. I wasn't worried about him; he could swim all day and had done 10,000-meter swims before. I returned to the beach and gave the lifeguard Rick's message and sat back down on my poncho liner. The lifeguard demanded to know where Rick was going and what I was going to do. So I told him. My buddy was swimming to the green ship and I was going to do nothing. Rick was a big boy and I had told him not to do it. I planned to sit here with my binoculars and watch him.

After the frustrated lifeguard had called the MPs, he pestered me about Rick. Soon I could no longer see Rick as he crested the waves. I was a little concerned but soon saw that he was still swimming. By this time the lifeguard was going nuts because the MPs hadn't started yet and he didn't think anyone could swim that far. There was one other concern that I hadn't mentioned yet. Just three miles from this area was the third most shark-infested waters in the world. He asked how I knew Rick was still OK. I handed him my binoculars and told him to look around the deck of the ship, where men were lined up cheering Rick on and waving him forward. The MPs were now heading out; I suppose they had finally gotten all the equipment together. Now I was cheering for Rick. I knew he was going to get in trouble but I wanted him to reach the ship so the MPs couldn't claim they kept him from drowning.

It was going to be real close. The guys on the boat were jumping up and down now, shouting at Rick to hurry and pointing to the MPs in the Zodiac headed that way. Rick had just made it up on the boat tie-up platform when the MPs pulled up. Before they could say anything, Rick said, "Man, I'm glad to see you guys. I'm too tired to swim back. Mind if I catch a ride with you?" With that he waved good bye to the guys on the ship and came back to the beach with the MPs. The lifeguard banned him from the beach for two weeks. After only 20 minutes Rick was back. The lifeguard was naturally upset until I gave my assurance that Rick would not be allowed near the water even if we as a group had to tackle him and tie him up. That night at the staff meeting, when the Major asked if there was anything he needed to know, everyone just pointed to Rick. It was quite amusing watching Rick explain to the Major how he got banned from the beach.

CROOKED COPS

We were permitted to go to the other side on weekends or weekdays if there was business to conduct and we needed to stay overnight. I had signed for several safe houses on both sides of Panama for team members to stay in without cost. On the day before MSG Graham was to leave, during the half-hour drive back I was stopped three times by police. The first time I was the next to the last vehicle and the only gringo in line. The cop told me I was speeding. Without a word I handed him my license and a $10 bill. He thanked me and I drove off. The second time was just before what Check Point Charlie. The cop waved me over and told me I was doing 60K in a 35K zone. I asked to see his radar but he replied that his eye was calibrated and he was specially trained. He then added that for $50 I would not have to go to court where it would cost me $100 or more. We settled on $10 and once more I drove off. Was I was hot! That second cop really needed a butt-kicking. Then the third cop stopped me. Again I was the only gringo in line. As he came to me I didn't even bother with my license but simply handed him my last $10. I then asked Jeff if I could borrow $2 so I could eat. The cop asked if I was kidding when I asked my friend for money to eat with. I showed him my empty wallet. When I told him I needed $1.85 to eat in the mess hall, he gave me back $2. At least I found one which was not quite as crooked as others. We laughed about it at dinner that night.

SOME DIFFICULT LETTERS

For a family man, one of the most difficult tasks is writing letters to be sent if he fails to return. Anyone who has done so can empathize. The thoughts that come while writing serve as a reminder of the very special things in life. Three times while writing Nissa's letter I had to stop because of the acute pain. Why did I write those letters? Because we were increasingly convinced that the showdown was soon to come. We had been training for some extremely dangerous missions which, for the most part, I suppose remain classified to this day.

HUMAN PACK MULES, WITH A KICK

One of our training missions made us the most heavily loaded and dangerous ten men alive. I doubt we could have carried much more. As it was, our loads were so heavy we could take only short, awkward steps. Fortunately we would only need to walk 30 yards or so after getting off the choppers. Just how much were we carrying? About 180 pounds per man. Each wore a load carrying vest (LCV) with ten to fifteen 30-round magazines; a 120-round bandoleer of extra ammo; two to four grenades; a 9-mm pistol with two extra 15-round magazines; a knife; a compass; 2 x 1-quart canteen; half a VS-17 panel; a pen flare; a strobe light; and an MRE. On the average the vest weighed 70 pounds.

We also had the following weapons with ammunition, along with radios: *2 x M-19 60mm mortars with 24 rounds per gun; *1 x 90mm recoilless rifle with 14 rounds; *2 x M-24 sniper systems with 100 rounds per gun; *2-M60 machine guns with 1 extra barrel per gun. Each gunner carried 500 rounds and the two snipers carried an additional 1500 rounds for each M-60. Also there were two claymore mines; two PRC-126 radios; one SATCOM radio; an M-16A2 per man except for the two snipers.

At rehearsal it took us 4½ minutes to fire the bulk of what we carried, all the mortar and 90-mm rounds, 1600 rounds from each of the M-60s, 50 sniper rounds per gun. Then we changed the two red-hot machine gun barrels and moved out. We ran a specified distance to a chainlink fence, tied the two claymore mines on the fence, and moved to the left and right about 30 feet, firing them back toward the enemy while blowing an escape hole in the fence. About 50 men from 7th ID watched from a distance. While they laughed as we got off the choppers because we couldn't run very fast with these loads, their mouths hung open when we finished. They had no idea how much or how fast we could fire and engage the targets. I can't specify the exact mission but it was typical of what we faced and compelled us to write letters to our wives and kids. We felt that if we got in on the ground we would have about 10 minutes to do our damage before the PDF could start mounting a counter attack.

One member I must mention is, the company mechanic, SGT Vic Routen, who had volunteered to be the assistant 90-mm gunner if the mission went down. Use of anyone without an MOS of 18 was unauthorized but there was a crucial shortage. Initially a big burley rigger was asked to volunteer but when he was told the mission, he almost cried and refused to go. SGT Routen agreed to go but professed to not know anything about the 90-mm. With one of us training him, he practiced until he became probably one of the best assistant 90-mm gunners in the Army. He was a fine young soldier who always helped whenever he could. Another man worth mentioning was SP4 Mario Rivera, the other parachute rigger, who accompanied one of the teams as translator once the missions started.

There was another mission that would have caused us to write letters. Two sniper teams were assigned to cover an airfield in case certain individuals attempted to escape. Given the lack of vegetation in that area, if one team fired on a target the only way to escape when the enemy reacted, was for the other team to fire on the enemy going after the first team. This would continue until we could back out. How well would this have worked? We felt it would only delay the inevitable outcome. Fortunately our scheme was never tested since that particular mission was aborted. Chief Bush and I were to have been one of the sniper teams.

CERTIFICATION

SF Certification was conducted this month. It was accomplished in three days but anyone in SF will tell you this is no fun. We had already completed the shooting aspects of certification, which is how we did it in three days. First was the APFT, where a score of 80% or better was required for each event. Next was the swim test at the lagoon on Fort Sherman. The rest of the day was spent on Army Common Task Testing, Day 2, a very rough day. First the 12K day land navigation was done with 55 pounds in the ruck, plus weapons and water. After lunch was Special Forces Common Task Testing. That night was the 12k night land navigation with the same load as the day's. Day 3 was SF MOS testing. And that night came the dreaded 32K/20-mile ruck march in less than seven hours carrying the same weight as during land navigation. After having done all these activities in a period of three days, waking the following morning was agony. We joked later that if JUST CAUSE had occurred in the three or four days afterward, the mission would have had to wait on us. Many toenails are lost after this rigorous affair. I've always had one or two drop off a few weeks later.

MAKING GRENADES

We had very few grenades. With the growing belief that JUST CAUSE would soon occur, SGM Stone, Rick Lazaras and I decided to make some if none could be obtained through the supply system. Empty soup cans, beer cans and coke cans packed with C4 and nails were to serve as grenades. While Stoney and Rick were packing, I was cutting and timing fuses, then putting the caps and fuse lighters on the fuse. At the same time we watched the TV. Noriega was on TV; once he even pointed to a map, announcing the presence of American commandos training in his country to capture him. I looked to see where he was pointing. Doggone if he wasn't pointing at Battery Pratt! Wonder what he would have said had he known we were inside making grenades.

RICK'S HOT DATE

One afternoon Rick Lazaras asked if he could borrow one of the Army 2½-ton trucks that evening. I asked why and he said he had a date with a gal from 7th ID. I extracted a promise that he would not drive the truck off post before I okayed it. A little later I saw him place some honeycomb material in the back of the truck. I knew what he was making: a bed in the back of the truck. I asked him for his intended parking place but he merely grinned and wouldn't divulge the information. Later that night, while outside, I heard a 2½-ton truck coming uphill. Rather than turning into the battery it went left up the hill to an old WW II shoreline watchtower. It had to be Rick. A couple of the others who knew of Rick's plans walked with me to the end of the road and we sneaked up the hill. On nearing Rick's location, we crept to where we could hear them then we waited. As soon as things heated up we made weird sounds and shook some bushes. The frightened woman asked Rick about the noises. Rick shouted at the sorry SOBs to go home and leave them alone! We were cracking up laughing but decided to cut him some slack. As we left we cautioned them not to stay out too late!

"OPERATION JUST CAUSE" - PANAMA

RECALL, 17 DECEMBER 1989

On the night of December 17th of 1989 several of us were watching TV in the Bat Cave. Some were at Fort Davis or at one of the five safe houses on Fort Espinar. There were also about six single guys in downtown Colon. The company always had one or two people who actually knew everyone's true location, regardless of what senior leadership of the company had been told. This was because of the many rules about where we could go and what time we should be back or at one of the safe houses. That night I was one of those who knew.

Around 2300 hours MAJ Perez told me to call the safe houses and have everyone come in. I asked why and he said a recall was being done because the situation had deteriorated for Americans off post and he wanted everyone back before the 2400 curfew. His wish presented a slight problem: he thought everyone was at the safe houses. He was blissfully unaware of the six single guys who, against orders, were spending the night at a place down town. This was no time for evasion. I said someone who could pass as Spanish must be sent in a rental vehicle downtown to the club and have the guys return. He said, disbelieving, "No! We don't have anyone there!"

When he was finally convinced we chose Chief Bush. This task was incredibly dangerous. Chief would be alone, accompanied only by a 9-mm pistol for protection. But if anyone could pull it off, he could. Our plan, as it turned out, proved to be unnecessary.

The woman who ran the club had once been married to a Special Forces man and still had some affection for SF guys. She had overheard one of the PDF men tell his buddies that things had turned bad. They planned to await the arrival of reinforcements before arresting the gringos. She told one of our men then sneaked them to the back by ones and twos and out the back door. When Chief got there she told him what she had done and he safely returned. Everyone made it back by 2400 hours. Our system had worked.

On the morning of 18 Dec 1989 we were told we would soon be moving to Albrook Air Force Base on the other side of Panama that night. We were certain this was no false alarm; we had been training diligently and planning potential operations. I had also requested additional ammunition to round out the areas of shortage. What prompted all our preparation? What made us so sure this was the real thing? The situation in Panama had deteriorated considerably over the past few months. In August Fidel Castro, his brother Raul, and the Nicaraguan Minister of Defense held a meeting in Rio Hato with LTC Gonzo Gonzolez, commander of the Panamanian Special Forces, the Mancho de Mante. No one knew why but it wasn't a barbecue. Assaults on Americans by police and members of the Dignity Battalion had increased significantly. Members of the Dignity Battalion were called the Ding Bats because most were stupid and all were thieves and criminals. The Ding Bats caused numerous problems. They were suspected of having fired random shots at Americans in the last few months. Additionally, Panamanian citizens who worked for the US were constantly harassed. Drugs moving through the canal were on the increase and everyone knew of Noriega's involvement. There were reports of large sums of counterfeit American dollars being shipped to Panama for distribution in the U.S.

THE WARNING ORDER

This morning we were given the warning order that we were moving to the other side, to a mission support site (MSS) at AlBrook AFB. We were told that come night we would be fly on three CH-47s. We began packing our equipment, drawing up ammunition lists and making preparations. There was much debate about this being a false alert. Those of us a little older than the rest knew chances were it would be for real very soon; we just didn't know how soon. So much ammunition and demolitions were assembled at the Bat Cave that we could not take it all. There were three CH-47s for 45 men and whatever else we could get on board. Still, quite a bit was left behind, which was fine because later someone else would need it and would get it.

19 December 1989
HANGAR 450

At Albrook AFB we were in hanger 450 with 3rd Battalion of 7th Special Forces Group. Having been alerted so often over the last two years, they were convinced it was another phony alert. They hadn't the access to intelligence our company had from the Bat

Cave, although their commanders did at the nightly staff meetings. Meanwhile no one could, or would, say when it was going to happen. While waiting we assisted by establishing fighting and security positions around the hanger. A shower point was also constructed because we didn't know how long we would be there.

FINAL INDICATOR

At 1500 hours two 5-ton trucks pulled up in front of the hanger. An SFC got out of the front truck and asked for SFC Johnson; I identified myself. He then informed me that there was ammunition for me in the trucks. I climbed in the back of one. Oh my gosh, I thought as I counted, 30 M72 light anti-tank weapons (LAW), 24 AT-4 anti-tank weapons, 240 40-mm grenades and 220 hand grenades. Why me, I asked. He replied, "This is the stuff the boss said you requested for the operation if it went down". If this doesn't go down, I thought, I'm going to be turning ammunition in long after everyone else has gone back to Fort Bragg! I sighed and asked where to sign? His reply shocked me. "You don't sign. The boss said to tell you you're going to be using this stuff before morning." I quickly showed some of the guys where to unload the stuff and took off to find SGM Stone. When I found him I asked him to step aside for a moment; I had something very important to tell him. He asked what was so important. I quickly told him, "It's going down tonight." There's a good chance it will, he agreed. NO, I countered, I mean it is going down tonight for sure. He asked, "What makes you so sure it's going down tonight?" "Because I was just given a quarter-million dollars' worth of munitions and didn't have to sign for the stuff! The guy's boss, the SOUTHCOM G4, had him tell me we would be using it before morning! SGM Stone looked at me then said, "Let's go find the Major." Before we could, COL Jacobly came out and called everyone over to a table in the middle of the hanger.

THE WORD COMES DOWN

I glanced at my watch as we gathered around: it was around 1600 hours. Everyone had an opinion about what it was about. Some speculated that we would be told we could go back home and so on. COL Jacobly climbed up on a table and had everyone move closer. Keep in mind he chewed tobacco. His briefing was something like this: All right gentleman! For those of you who don't know me (spit). I'm COL Jacobly the SOCSOUTH Commander (spit). Those that know me will tell you (spit) that when I tell you it's no bull (spit) then its no bull! (spit) Fellows I'm telling you now (spit) if the Panamanians don't start it by 0100 in the morning, WE ARE! It got very quite then and a most serious air settled in among us. By now we knew there would be fighting that night and some of us might not be alive the next morning. The biggest skeptics had strange looks on their faces. We spent the rest of the day rechecking equipment. Missions would come down and then they would be changed.

Around 2300 we got word that the mission for which we had trained so hard and which left us little time on target had been changed. We later joked that they had decided our ten-man SF team was overkill so they decided to send a Ranger Battalion instead. Someone decided that ODA 713 and 715 would flank a warehouse reported to store 6 to 12 B-100 armored vehicles. If they attempted to break out or began to fire before 7th Infantry Division Armor arrived, we were to engage them. With that we picked up two AT-4s per man and reviewed firing procedures. Ski looked at me and I said, "Clank, clank, I'm a tank," then shook my head. He chuckled, claming this could be like kicking over a big bee's nest. After that we all got quiet with our private thoughts.

20 DECEMBER 1989: THE FIRST SHOTS ARE FIRED

It was around 0035 hours, people were moving around and choppers were cranking up. Everyone was wearing their gear and preparing to move out. Chief and I were planning our exit through the wire when suddenly bullets were flying everywhere: the Panamanians had fired first. They had driven a bus down the road just outside the perimeter fence and had fired on us. Fortunately their aim with their AK47s was high and they and missed everyone. COL Jacobly had a close call. He was upstairs pointing to his map board briefing someone when the first shots were fired; two went through his map board. Those MPs at the gate deserved medals. When the first shots were fired they pulled their Humvee into the road and opened up on that bus. A few days later I looked at the bus; its front was full of holes. Immediately after the first shots, from the general area of the service company inside the hanger rounds could be heard being chambered into weapons. Everyone had gotten down; our M60s could be heard outside returning fire. But another sound sent shivers down my spine. I called out, "713, STAY DOWN, grab your gear and follow me." Before we could get started more bullets were soon coming out of the hanger than was coming in. The team crawled outside and rolled into a concrete drainage ditch. When the firing came under control, we went back in.

In the middle of the hangar COL Jacobly was shouting at everyone to launch. The choppers were winding up for liftoff, men were moving with purpose. We returned to the room we had been in and retrieved the AT4s. We had joined with another team for a total of 12 men. Then we exited into the night and soon were on our way, moving quickly across the airfield to the fence. Out came the 18-inch bolt cutters; minutes later an opening was made in the fence. Once through the fence we separated into two six-man teams for bilateral target observation. While moving into position our team came under intense fire from the rear. In a matter of six or seven seconds about 200 tracer rounds landed around us. One team member found a bullet hole through his uniform the next morning. I noted the direction of the fire and got on the radio. "10, 10 this is 13. CEASE FIRE, CEASE FIRE, you're raining on us! 13, this is 10. We have bad guys in the wire and can't stop at this moment. 10, this is 13, for God's sake, find out who's out of position and please get them back. We can't stand much more without getting hit."

For the next three hours we held this position, repeatedly coming under different types of fire. To the right was someone with a 7.62 machine gun, firing a long burst or two every 15 to 20 minutes then going silent. We would look up and watch the tracers about 40 feet overhead. He never seemed to change his aim or elevation. On the hillside in front were two armored vehicles, firing at each other a few minutes with 50 cal then maneuvering. Shortly after that their firing at each other would resume. After several tracers had passed close by, I asked Chief to crawl forward and find us a better place. He had gone about 10 feet when a 50-cal tracer passed right to left about 5 feet in front. He quickly put it in reverse and scooted backward. Then he called out to me, "Hey, Pop! I think we should stay here for a little bit!" I then instructed everyone to find a tire track and get in the bottom of it. Based on the situation, the guys were positioned so that three were looking forward and three backward.

In front were three or four heavy firefights. Then there were mortar rounds that landed not too far to our front. Several times I radioed 10 for permission to attack the target; each time I was told to hold our position. Our situation had significantly worsened; 50-cal tracers were passing between us. With that I had the men saddle up and follow me to a safer location. We retreated about 30 yards or so and positioned ourselves in a ditch. While the view wasn't as good, we were a heck of a lot safer. At last 7th ID Armor arrived at the warehouse and we were ordered to return to the MSS. The return was scary. As we moved through the wire I was concerned about young soldiers from Service Company firing us up. Before going through the wire I had radioed that we were coming in and asked SGM Stone to go up and down the line once to let them know that friendlies were coming in. The guys were spread out left and right so that if someone fired, they wouldn't hit two men.

20 December 1989
PECORA RIVER BRIDGE

On entering the hangar we were told that A/3/7th SF had ambushed Battalion 2000 at the Pecora River Bridge. There was no radio contact after the ambush; everyone was concerned that those 30 men had run into overwhelming odds. We knew those men. Their last message had stated they were landing and had spotted the convoy. We knew they had fire support from an AC-130, a flying gun platform with the remarkable ability to fire accurately where needed. Although no one said so out loud, I think we were all worried that the worst had occurred. We all had friends in that company and two of our men (SGTs Landis and Woodall) were with them. For once these SF men made no wise crack; in fact, no one was talking.

I instructed the men to stack the AT-4s for the most part and grab some extra ammunition for the guys at the bridge. In moments we were out the back door to board the choppers that were revving up. There can be humor in any situation. COL Jacobly and LTC Wilderman were standing beside one chopper, arguing about who could or couldn't go to the bridge with the relief force. Their conversation went something like this. "COL, you can't go out there, you know too much. We can't afford to have something happen to you." "LTC, I don't care! Those are my men and they're in trouble." "Sir, you can't go and you know it. Send me I'll make sure you get the word as soon as we link up." "No you can't go. This is their operation; you or I would get in the way. We both have too much rank." "Look, sir, I'll not get in the way. You let me go out there and I'll just be a private. You can tell them my rank is invalid out there. I just want the chance to fight beside these guys. You know I'll probably never get another chance."

I intervened. "COL, if he leaves his rank here I'll take him on my team as another gun." The COL asked, "Are you sure?" I said, "Yes sir." He then turned to LTC Wilderman and said, "OK, but you're under his control. He tells you you're using your rank, you back off. You got it?" "Yes, sir, thanks!" LTC Wilderman then promised me he would be the best junior weapons man I ever had. And that was how LTC Wilderman got on the chopper. We were now ready to board. There were more people on those birds than I thought possible. I think there were 16 or 17 fully loaded combat soldiers on each UH-60. Everyone managed to get in. Heck, we were sitting on each other's feet, in other guy's laps, any way we could get on. Except for SGM Stone. He had been directing people to their birds and now there was no room anywhere, almost. David (Ski) Thomaleski was sitting in the door of one bird. Ski was no little guy at 5 feet 11 inches and 220 pounds, and a 32-inch waist. Ski called to SGM Stone to jump on his lap, and he would hold him in until we got there. SGM Stone, not being real big at 5 feet 8 inches, shrugged his shoulders and jumped up. Ski wrapped one of his big arms around Stoney. We gave the thumbs-up signal and the choppers lifted off for the bridge.

The flight to the bridge was about 30 minutes. In the gray of dawn we could suddenly see the bridge. The chopper started the descent but wasn't yet on the ground before we started jumping off. As we started forward to secure the wood line several of the guys from A/3/7 appeared. It turned out they were all OK but for some unknown reason whoever they were talking to in the rear had not been relaying their messages to command. They did have a problem, though. They weren't strong enough to chance crossing the bridge and splitting their forces. With that the commanders on the ground decided that our company would go across and secure/clear the other side. That is, as soon as the bridge was cleared underneath.

ENEMY UNDER THE BRIDGE
While still dark, the Panamanians had tried to mount a counterattack and had charged across the bridge. This effort turned out badly for them because SFC Woodall was there with a 5.56mm SAW and two others had M16s. Together they ate the Panamanians' lunch. One Panamanian dove 20 feet over the side of the bridge to avoid the massive rain of bullets. In doing so he sustained a round in the leg and on landing broke that same leg. Keep in mind, it was still dark and no one could tell how many were under the bridge.

The river wasn't deep enough to keep them from wading across and attacking. The injured Panamanian would occasionally make a noise and someone would pitch a grenade under the bridge. By now it was daylight and we wanted to cross the bridge, so it had to be cleared underneath. A couple guys pitched grenades. As soon as the grenades exploded, five or six men rushed underneath and found the guy. Because he had lain flat, no grenade fragment had hit him. He wasn't entirely lucky, though. His leg had required treatment for too long. The medics did what they could and he was flown out. But we learned later that he had lost the leg. I learned years latter this man was the brother-inlaw of one of the men from 3/7, Mike Stangle.

Before anyone crossed I fired an AT-4 into the lead truck; someone might have decided to wait there and fire on us as we crossed. I lost some of my hearing when I fired because my earplug had fallen out. Then the teams started across. There was a body on the roadway. On approaching the body, one man in front of me kicked it to make sure the guy wasn't playing possum. When he kicked it a third time I said, "Hey! The guy's dead! Move on, you're disturbing the flies!" He said, "You can't be sure of that." I said, "Look, there is no way a person can lie still while 50 flies are crawling on his face and there is no way to fake rigor mortis. The guy is stiff as a board." He said I'd be sorry if the guy jumped up and shot someone but he finally moved on.

SNIPER IN THE WINDOW

As the sniper I covered the movement of the men clearing the buildings on the right while I watched the rear of the buildings for escaping PDF. With me was SSG Bill Wester and watching the shot-up and abandoned vehicles in the road was SFC Rick Lazaras. To the right was a stone quarry, with three buildings on the left and a small house 50 yards up the hill. The gravest danger lay in the numerous gravel piles, items of heavy equipment, and ditches that ran throughout the yard. At one point the men thought an enemy sniper had been spotted in the building 50 yards up the hill. The team leader wanted to fire him up but you fight a sniper with a sniper. I moved into what I thought was a good position and scoped for the target. I saw him and started to fire but something didn't look right. The team leader was pressing for permission to fire but I asked the company commander to delay it a moment. I moved in closer and looked through my scope again.

It was an old man standing back from the window with a broom in his hand. The leader of the clearing team tried to tell the company commander that I was screwed up and couldn't distinguish a rifle from a broom. Chief Bush broke in on my side of the argument and told the company commander he and a couple of guys would move closer if I could cover them. I said, "You're covered". MAJ Perez told them to go for it. As they approached the house in short rushes, the old man came out. Turned out he was a retired American living there and working as the site manager. Until we told him, the old man didn't realize how close he had come to dying that day. Once that position was cleared, SSG Wester, SFC Lazaras and I cleared the seven trucks in the roadway.

We then positioned ourselves to cover ODA 714, MSG Lazano's team, as they cleared the house and evacuated the family. With that the others and I moved to the next house. Here it got a little more interesting. Some of the men went to the front of the house while SGT O'Brian and I circled to the rear. As we approached the rear we spotted movement. He looked at me and I motioned him forward. We moved up and caught eight soldiers burning their uniforms and military identification cards. A search of the house yielded two weapons. We were getting a little stretched thin now so we put out security and I led a couple of men to search the trucks. The trucks were loaded with equipment and some interesting items. We had captured 81-mm mortars, 90-mm recoilless rifles, 7.62 MAG 58 medium machineguns, 7.62 1919A6 medium machinegun, German light anti-tank weapons, rucksacks, 7.62x39 AK-47 rifles, pistols, ammunition for the above weapons, and one 50-pound drum of CS powder, (tear gas). In the rucksacks there were civilian clothes and 12-inch rubber hoses with weights in the ends. We loaded all this onto the only truck left running.

TWO MORE POWs

Afterward I walked back to Chief Bush. There was little else we could do and he needed someone there because he was alone. Not knowing how long we would stay, we made ourselves comfortable. SSG

Wester walked up. We were talking about events of the last 24 hours when SSG Wester looked up and saw two guys with machetes moving out of the brush to one of the houses cleared earlier. The three of us started toward the house. Wester was moving up the left side, Chief up the middle, and I was moving up the right. As we approached the two guys came from behind the house and attempted to reenter the woodline. I whistled and Chief called them over to him in Spanish. They started his way holding their machetes. Chief ordered them to drop the machetes. One did but the one in front continued forward, machete still in hand. Chief repeated the order but the guy was still talking, and coming forward. By now he was 20 feet away. Chief started to tell him again but I felt the guy was too close already. I shouldered my rifle and fired about 12 inches in front of his foot. That guy couldn't throw that machete down fast enough.

A split second after I fired that warning shot a second shot rang out just over the bank down by the road. I wondered what they were shooting at but I had more pressing issues. I told Wester to keep an eye on the tree line in case there were more. About then several guys from the company ran forward. The Captain asked what had happened? I told him but he interrupted, "You mean you were sleeping and got attacked!" I told him he was wrong and he repeated his accusation. By now I was mad so I asked how the hell he could know since he had been down on the roadway.

He then stepped between the prisoners and me and demanded to know if they were PDF. "You PDF! You PDF!" He shrieked. I interjected calmly, "Hey, that was John Wayne in the Green Berets. Try asking them in Spanish. That's what you went to school for." Then he asked if the prisoners had been searched. The two PDF wore only their underwear. Where, I asked, did he think they were hiding something. He replied, "You gotta be careful." I turned one around, bent him over and pointed to a large softball size hole in the guy's underwear. "Where do you think he's hiding something?" Several of the men laughed. I said to the CPT, "If you want to take credit for catching them, you can take them down to the Major." He trotted off happily with his two POWs.

One of the men from the captain's team asked if I had heard the shot from their location. "Yea," I replied, "what was that about?" It seems that when I had fired the warning shot at the man with the machete, the captain fired a wild shot that almost hit SSG Tomaleskie. When Ski was asked, he confirmed it; the shot reportedly missed him by a foot at most.

An hour later we got word to return to the bridge and prepare for departure. A US Sheridan tank had arrived to observe the bridge and MAJ Higgens had called for the choppers for our 18 POWs and us. Were we happy to see the two CH 53s! We somehow managed to get everyone on board then flew back to hangar 450.

A SPECIAL WHISKEY DECANTER

At Allbrook AFB someone had brought in Noriega's Cadillac limousine. SSG Wester and I checked it. The windshield had been shattered so we could reach in and unlock the door. After looking around inside I retrieved a cut glass whiskey decanter as a souvenir; this decanter, with other items, was later donated to the Airborne and Special Operations Museum in Fayetteville, North Carolina. We rested there the rest of the day; that was the first 24 hours of OPERATION JUST CAUSE for us. Had a camera been available those first hours, much of what we had witnessed would have been documented pictorially. Regrettably there were only my notes.

21 December 1989

The next day was spent in preparation for the move to Rio Hato in the afternoon. During the day we were subjected to sniper fire. Once even COL Jacobly got involved. The hangar sustained a couple of rounds and we snipers were trying to locate the enemy sniper through our scopes. Meanwhile the COL ran next door to an armor unit but the only one there was a private, who was working on an M113 APC. The COL asked if the APC was functional and could he could drive it. The private answered yes and the COL climbed in. With that they charged across the airfield. At the fence the COL ordered the private to drive through it, which he did. Unfortunately the COL had forgotten to secure the hatch in the open position. As the fence was hit, WHAM! The latch struck the COL on the head, nearly knocking him out. The private immediately realized he needed to turn around because the COL was hurt.

Everyone had some good laughs about it later, the COL included.

We flew out to Rio Hato from where we would spear head 7th ID's movements in the western part of the country. Two operations were planned for the following day. Rio Hato was an interesting place, having served as home of the Panamanian Special Forces, the Macho de Mante, their military academy and an armored recon unit. The Rangers had hit it hard; anti-personnel mines were still strewn about. What a great place to explore! I found some souvenirs: a bugle, a chrome engraved machete, an AK-47 bayonet, and a couple of other small items. I was greatly disturbed by the Rangers' and 7th ID's apparent disregard for the wealth of intelligence information available. There was a final commo log entry at 2330 hours on the 19th noting the American would attack at 0100 hours in the morning. An overlay showed rally points en route to Panama City. There were photographs of Fidel Castro and his brother at Rio Hato just four months before. There were unit manning rosters. It was a intelligence gold mine just laying around.

22 December 1989
SANTIAGO, PANAMA
This morning the company launched for Santiago. First the airfield was to be secured. I was aboard the lead bird swooping into the airfield. In the briefing we all agreed there would be no shooting unless it proved to be necessary. As the choppers went in I spotted a guard in a booth and told SFC Makar of

the possible target. I also informed SFC Demateo, on my left. I instructed both of them to keep the men left and right, with the middle clear if I needed to shoot. With the chopper still four or five feet from the ground, I shoved myself out the doorway. I hit the ground, ran twenty or thirty feet, then dropped down while raising my sniper rifle, the cross hairs focused on the guard. I could see him clearly, his hand just inches away from the holstered weapon. I fervently hoped he would not reach for the weapon; at that range he'd be dead before the weapon could be drawn.

The guard nervously watched our approach. There was another man with him; I doubted that I could get both. Our men were closing in; it was time to force the two PDF to get down, allowing us safe passage through the last 20-30 yards. I raised my crosshairs to the top of the windowsill and fired. The two guards dropped to the floor where they remained until they were captured without another shot. The unit then totally secured the airport. Vehicles were hot-wired and moved into positions to block the entrances. MAJ Perez then called the quartel in town. He informed them that they had 20 minutes to assemble their men in the center of the yard, lock all weapons in the arms room, and raise a white flag up the flagpole. What if they didn't, they asked. MAJ Perez had them go outside and look up. Back on the phone he told them that AC-130 would level their building, with them inside, if they didn't. That was the first ever MA BELL Operation.

SSG Jessie Wolf, CPT Wallace and I remained at the airfield with several prisoners while the company accepted surrender by the quartel. On their approach one of the PDF fired a pistol several times. He soon realized the folly of his actions. One of our men, armed with a 40-mm grenade launcher was sitting in the door of the chopper. On spotting the man who was firing, he put a round down his way. That was all it took; the man threw his pistol down and ran back inside. Two bullet holes were later found on the chopper.

The afternoon was wild. In gratitude the townspeople came out en masse. They were singing and shaking each man's hand. Some reporters had come from Costa Rica to interview some of my men. Just then a car pulled up at the gate. A Panamanian got out cursed us and said he was a big Noriega supporter. The crowd surged forward and savagely beat him and his car. He was then thrown back in his car, which was then pushed into a ditch. I asked the reporter why that had not been filmed. Why wasn't he documenting the Panamanian people's support for us? I cautioned him against speaking with any of our people. He was the press, he declared, and had a right to talk to the soldiers. Making sure his camera was off, I warned him, I would inform the crowd of his loyalty to Noriega if he did. With that I called and waved to the crowd, which started them cheering. I then strongly encouraged the reporter to join the crowd on the other side of the street, which he did.

That evening we returned to Rio Hato from where, during the next few days, several missions were flown. This process was repeated many times. Secure a place close by and give them a phone call. The company went into Chitre, El Valle, Los Tables, Penonome and other places. Later I will relate unique stories from some.

23 December 1989

Today we attempted to capture LTC Gonzo Gonzales and would have succeeded had it not been for 7th ID. One of our team members, who was observing his girlfriend's apartment, reported the presence of someone who resembled Gonzales. In minutes we were ready to go. One problem: today we didn't have the Task Force 160 birds so we had to depend on 7th ID for chopper support. They refused to provide the choppers until they could assemble a task force to assist us. Thirty of us were ready now but 7th ID needed almost four hours. At the apartment we discovered that Gonzales was missed by two hours. Every man in the company was furious.

24 December 1989

CHRISTMAS EVE IN SANTIAGO

This afternoon my team switched out with another in Santiago. What we found there was most disturbing. Only 20 pounds of flour and 10 pounds of beans were available to feed the prisoners, who numbered more than 170. It was 4 p.m. on Christmas Eve. While interviewing some of the prisoners, I found that they had had almost nothing to eat for some time. What to do? Chief Bush, Wynne and I together

67

devised a heck of a plan. If the plan worked, few in this town would soon forget this Christmas Eve!

We would appeal to the townsfolk, our theme being that the war over and Christmas was a time for forgiveness. Chief very effectively convinced the people that donating foodstuff would go far in healing past wounds. Meanwhile the Law of War manual was our moral authority to open a couple of charge accounts for food for the prisoners. We sent Wynne to ask the merchants for a line of credit. Not only did he do this, he also persuaded some suppliers to donate. We were relieved to find that we could open the charge accounts. Things were looking up. A dozen local ladies volunteered to prepare the Christmas Eve meal.

By 6:00 PM we had plenty of food: 70 chickens, 400 pounds of beans and rice, 100 pounds of flour, a side of beef in the freezer, one cow still on the hoof in the courtyard along with some chickens and a turkey. Even the Pepsi and Coke distributors each donated 25 cases of soft drinks. Tim was appointed to be in charge of the kitchen and local accounts; he did an excellent job. Dinner that night was truly fantastic. The evening was memorable; several prisoners apologized for their actions of the past year. Everyone thanked us for finally removing Noriega from office.

25 December 1989

One lady in Santiago was tremendously helpful. She had persuaded several of the others to help and was there every day. She was previously an English teacher but under Noriega had been arrested once and beaten. She was quite a lady, Irma del C of Fabrega, Santiago, Veraguas, Panama. All Mrs. Fabrega asked in return was when we got back to the US, that I call her sister in Texas and let her know that Mrs. Fabrega was OK. I did this when we got back in mid January and spoke with her and her family. They were James and Martha Wright of Grand Prairie, Texas.

Christmas day was quiet. While SSG Luis Vasquez and I were talking, a Panamanian officer asked if he could speak with us in private. We went to his office, where he told us that he had given a false name; he then gave his real name. He had been an officer in the Panamanian unit UESAT, which was to have come to the aid of Noriega on 4 Oct 89 when several Panamanian officers had attempted a coup. That day his unit was rushing to the scene when they were stopped and held on the Bridge of the Americas by American forces. Because of that he had been put out of UESAT and transferred to Santiago, after he had been brought before Noriega and forced to prove his allegiance or face death. He was certain the US wanted him. He requested permission to surrender to me in a small formal ceremony held in the office. SSG Vasquez first verified that he was indeed wanted; he was. A chopper was en route to pick him up. Before his surrender we went into his sleeping area where he gave us some of his military items. He reasoned that if he didn't, the PDF would steal them when he left. With that done we chatted until time to conduct the ceremony. I accepted his side arm. Before we went to wait on the chopper, he asked one other favor. After he had been in custody a few days, would I please call his wife to let her know he had survived. After giving it some thought, I said I would call for him.

I called home tonight to let my family know I was OK. After talking for 20 minutes Josie remarked that the phone call would surely cost a fortune. I assured her that I was calling from my office. "Your office?" "Yeah, I'm now the commander of police forces in Santiago and I'm sitting in the old commander's office, which is mine for the moment." We talked a few moments more. It was good to talk with her and the kids; I didn't know when I'd have another chance.

26 December 1989

LTC Trumbel came in the chopper today along with the team that was switching out with us. Chief Bush was to become pay master for 7th Special Forces accounts established throughout the western part of the country. With that we went back to Rio Hato for a day or two. At Rio Hato there was still plenty to do. A couple of motorcycles had been repaired by SGT Routen for transportation. We searched for additional weapons and other things. In the club we found a storage closet filled with booze. As booze was prohibited for U.S. forces in Panama, this was a bonus. When it was almost dark we took a vehicle in which to load the booze. Some vehicle! It was a small four-door Toyota, without doors, hood or trunk lid, and the top caved in deep enough that one could bathe in it. Stoney, Rick and I loaded everything we could get into the car and started our drive back. It was almost dark.

We were somewhat concerned over 7th ID's tendency to shoot often at almost anything. So we drove slowly. At the library, while we were unloading a warrant officer from 7th ID saw what we were doing. He ran off childishly saying threateningly, "I'm going to tell!" We had just finished making a table out of the cases, a couple of ponchos thrown on top with some items over these for camouflage. The 7th ID Battalion CSM walked in, as if he owned the place, looking for the booze. We endured his obnoxious behavior a while then MSG Rick Lazano asked, "What the hell are you doing and what do you want?" He informed us that we reportedly had booze and he was looking for it. Rick asked, "Do you see any? What's it to you? We aren't part of 7th ID. What right do you have to just walk in and start searching without talking with our SGM first?" He then demanded to know who Rick was; Rick told him. With that he stormed out to SGM Stone's office.

Stoney had just stored a couple of six packs in his refrigerator when the CSM came in. Of course Stoney had to feign surprise. No one behaved irresponsibly with the stuff. Everyone stayed within the limit: two beers or one mixed drink, and only in the evening. When we moved back to Battery Pratt all the booze came back with us. That's a story I'll tell later.

EL VALLE
The mission to El Valle is worth mentioning. We flew out of Rio Hato, before first light, heading north into the mountains to the town of El Valle. The ride was exhilarating! We flew over the water with the

birds, at times so low that water spray splashed over our boots and stung our faces. Then we turned toward the mountains. Our plan was simple: we would land and seize the tourist hotel. Then we would call the small military garrison in town and tell them it was time to surrender. We landed, secured the hotel, then MAJ Perez attempted to call. He couldn't get through, though, because the phone was dead. We got back on the choppers to find the garrison but all we found was the police station, so we landed there. The little clearing proved to be a tight fit for the bird but it landed.

We soon discovered why we couldn't find the garrison. Evidently the townspeople had decided on Christmas Eve to give themselves a present. Having grown tired of waiting for us, they burned the garrison to the ground and chased the soldiers away. Afterwards they went to the mayor's house, kicked his butt, burned his house to the ground, and ran him out of town. The small Dignity Battalion cell left in town wisely took the hint and left on their own. That is, except for their leader. He was locked up in his own house and under guard by the towns people, waiting for us.

By now a crowd had gathered and the official town welcoming committee was arriving. They pulled up in two Jeep Cherokees loaded with two 10-gallon pots of freshly squeezed orange juice with ice and about 200 small sandwiches. Many of the people here had relatives in the US. One of the soldiers allowed to remain had information on a radio transmitter hidden in a house in the mountains. The house reportedly belonged to the COL, head of police for the city of Colon. We loaded the soldier into a chopper and flew to the house about 30 minutes away in some of the most mountainous country in Panama. We found the house but nowhere for the birds to land. So the pilots let us out on the roof, the wheels just over the crown and the chopper staying airborne. We exited onto the roof and slid down the back side to the ground. The radio was found with little trouble, and some weapons, too. Afterward we walked down the road for pickup by the chopper. We flew back to El Valle, searched a house on the hill, and returned to town. On our way out the townsfolk came with bags of fruit. Each man was given a large bag of oranges, tangerines, apples and bananas. The 7th ID showed up just before we left, entertaining the people with their three-second rushes as if taking a dangerous target. The locals were amused but. I pitied these young soldiers who were simply obeying orders. So many in the town thanked us and made us feel special about our mission.

December 1989
REAL FEAR
The ride back started peacefully. It was sunset and we were flying with the doors open. With the sun behind the horizon, the sky was still beautiful and things could not have been nicer. Suddenly the crew chief dove across everyone and jammed his fist down on the button to launch flares. Simultaneously the pilot jerked the chopper hard to the right into a dive. Only one thing could provoke such action: a surface-to-air missile (SAM)! Utter helplessness is having a

$2500 rifle in hand, knowing a missile is coming, yet unable to do more than watch for it! The pilot later said that his instruments had detected a SAM lock-on signal, although he wasn't sure it had been fired. I did gain a new respect for those guys flying.

CHITRE

Chitre was almost a firefight. We seized the airport just before daylight and MAJ Perez made the phone call. The commander was rousing his men to stand and fight. He was fourth on the list of the top-50 bad guys in Panama we most wanted to arrest. He knew he would be wanted for his suspected role in several murders and tortures so he boldly declared their intention to fight to the death. MAJ Perez ordered our cover AC to do a fly-over and convince them otherwise. The AC-130 wasn't available today; we had a fast mover. That pilot flew so low the TV antenna seemed to dislodge from the roof and some roof tiles were loosened.

After a 15-minute wait the phone rang. It was the XO of the quartel, calling to say that their commander had been arrested and jailed. He also made sure we knew that all the weapons were being locked up and the men being assembled. He requested 15 more minutes. MAJ Perez agreed and told us there would be no firefight; however, we were to be prepared for a trap. We landed inside the compound with one chopper and dispersed quickly to secure the LZ. Then the second chopper came in. We secured the perimeter and about 200 prisoners. With this accomplished we went through the buildings and flushed out those left inside. As everywhere else, the civilians came out to cheer us. Only those with a similar experience can understand the overwhelming feeling this evokes. The former commander was brought out of his cell and sent back to Albrook AFB for processing; his fate remains unknown to me.

It was nearly lunchtime so the Major allowed some of us to eat. We ate at the Dairy Queen down the street. Afterward the people inside would not allow us to pay. They were overjoyed to be rid of the crooks who had stolen from them and in gratitude paid for lunch. No matter where we went in this country people were enormously grateful. Why this was never publicized by the press is a mystery to me. We soldiers often wonder why the press generally behaves more like they are the enemy rather than our own countrymen!

When the situation had quieted down the MAJ selected six of us to remain: MSG Lazano, SFC Guerra, SSG Vasquez, SFC Demateo, another man, and me. With that the rest flew back to Rio Hato. The first order of business was deciding where to bunk. The officers club was available into which we moved some bunks. In doing so we were more secure because we were the sole occupants and could secure the doors from the inside. There was running water. We could plan and talk among ourselves and use the radio without being heard by the PDF. The air-conditioning was a bonus. That night we patrolled downtown using one of the local police vehicles and one of them as the driver. We found the town quiet and everyone friendly. Lazano and I spent several hours discussing our plans for the next day or two. Early the next morning we briefed our men then had Gurrea meet with the town leaders. Others stood at the gate speaking with those who had information. Those who knew of weapons caches, human rights violations and other serious crimes were brought to us. The information Vasquez and I received was later written on cards for rapid cross reference. On one set of cards was a person's name, where he was from, and an associated event. On the second set the event was written and any associated names. The third set documented an event or item, the area, and associated names. On each card was written the informant name. On the last set were written the source, the information provided, and the validity of the information. This primitive mechanism provided our database.

Guerra had befriended the owner of three radio stations in the area; this man would allow us to send messages to the public. With such an opportunity we crafted a PSYOPs message to Ding Bat Battalion members offering them the chance to surrender and register with us. Those who were innocent of serious crime would be released, free from worry about being hunted down. Our offer was well received; several surrendered almost as soon as the first ad was aired. We also announced to the people that our mission was not to overtake the country but rather to ensure that the government whom they elected could rule the country.

December 1989
A PANAMANIAN VICE PRESIDENT ARRIVES

We received a radio message one morning that one of the two Panamanian vice presidents was to come that day. We quickly developed a plan to ensure his safety. He was coming to have the officers swear allegiance to the new government. Everything proceeded without a hitch. I took photos of all the officers assigned to our location because many had came there after December 20th, before our arrival. These were suspected of fleeing from their crimes. When possible these men were identified and where they came from. As a result, a couple were arrested.

HERE COME THE COWBOYS!

The third day brought the 7th ID, who were most unwelcome. Around 10:00 a.m. what sounded like a full-scale battle erupted somewhere outside town. As bad as it sounded, it only lasted about 30 seconds. Our patrols were recalled and most of our 200 PDF were ordered to report to their barracks where they were to stay. Rick and I had no idea what was going on but were soon to find out. Within 10 minutes a massive cloud of smoke billowed above the southern end of town. We thought it was a burning vehicle. A call came in our radio. It was a company commander from 7th ID, who wanted his smoke identified. I informed him that his was the only mushroom-sized cloud on the horizon. He then requested clearance to come in. I gave him the go ahead but belatedly realized that something was amiss; the guy on the radio sounded strung out. I quickly ordered the gates opened and herded everyone, U.S. and Panamanian, inside the buildings. The two Panamanians at the gate were checked to make sure they did not even have their holsters.

I had just reentered the team room when a string of humvees roared rapidly through the gate. The vehicles slid to an abrupt halt at evenly spaced intervals and backed up against the wall. The men inside were waving their machine guns; two pulling a 105-mm cannon nearly ran me down. These two pulled into the courtyard and jammed on the brakes; men jumped out and started loading their 105s. What the hell is going on, Rick asked. Someone has to get them under control! I surveyed the room and remarked that it better be the most gringo-looking of us; I realized I was that gringo looking individual. I quickly stripped to my T-shirt and flung my hat to the corner. "Rick," I joked, "if I get shot, re-arm the Panamanians and waste these stupid suckers!"

I stepped outside and headed aggressively for the first soldier, cursing loudly and generally raising cane. I had to—I didn't know their challenge and password. The young soldiers, intimated into unquestioning obedience, nervously unloaded their weapons while I screamed at them. My behavior and age made them think I must be someone of high rank. When I found the CPT and SFC who were running the company, I yelled at them too and had them come to my office. Yeah, I know, CPTs outrank SFCs but this was a potentially explosive situation. A few minutes later they were at the door, requesting permission to enter. "What the hell were you guys doing," I demanded. "I want to know why you came in like gangbusters!" Apparently their battalion S2 had told them we were under constant fire, with looting and rioting in the streets. Shaking my head, I asked if they believed the enemy to be inside the compound. The shooting outside town was a live fire check of their weapons systems. I learned later that the CPT had climbed on top of his humvee and had said to men, "Prepare to earn your CIBs. We're going in hot." I then revealed my rank but I told them they weren't in charge until we left, hoping they were too embarrassed to realize it wasn't so.

NEW YEAR 1990

I spent a thankfully quiet New Year in Chitre. Our only celebration was gathering for a drink in the club/team room that night.

January 1990
WANT TO TAKE A RIDE IN MY CHOPPER?

We sent the photos taken when the VP was here to several places. Within a couple of hours Santiago replied that two of the guys had indeed conducted interrogations that were blatant human rights violations. These two were to be sent to Rio Hato. No problem; one of the two was very friendly, wanting a ride on one of our choppers. This was a good time to grant his wish. I casually mentioned that a chopper was flying me to Rio Hato and asked if he wanted to ride. Yes, yes! he replied eagerly. One down, one to go. The second was child's play. I only had to mention that his friend and I were going down to Rio Hato and he invited himself, if space was available. The three of us boarded the chopper. At Rio Hato I asked them to join me while the chopper was being refueled. After we had walked a few steps I asked them to wait while I went back to the chopper for a moment. I told the crew what was going on and asked them cover me while I cuffed the two. I then walked back to the two, drew my pistol, and ordered them to turn around, their hands behind them. I then told them they were being arrested for their actions in Santiago. Quick ties were wrapped around their wrists and they were led to headquarters. With that done I flew back to Chitre.

Our time in Chitre was nearing the end. Word came the next day to have our gear ready for return to Rio Hato. The chopper came for us that afternoon. I tried to negotiate a few more days from MAJ Perez so we could continue our good work. Heck, the civilians wanted Guerra to get out of the Army so he could be their mayor! Our information gathering was growing although the evidence was not sufficiently strong to arrest those individuals we knew to be guilty. One was named by several sources as handling weapons caches and drugs; we were closing in. The Major was sympathetic but declined my request, saying that things were drawing down and we needed to start closing back in. He did promise that I would be one of the first to go back to Battery Pratt to start getting things ready when 2nd Battalion was in country.

RIO HATO, AGAIN
At Rio Hato the "Weapons Buy Back" program was in full swing. A local asked if we would pay for

tanks. Sure, I said, if you have one or know where one is. He led me to a B-100 armored vehicle down an embankment. The rest of the day was spent extricating it from where it was located.

A RIDE TO DAVID

MAJ Perez asked if I wanted to ride to the town of David where ODA 716 was located. He didn't have to ask twice. At the airfield in David my sniper rifle was generating much curiosity. The M-24 sniper system was new so a number of people didn't know what it was. Before our departure, a C-130 did an impressive low-level fly-by. Not to be outdone, our chopper pilot told us to strap in; he was going to demonstrate the capabilities of the UH-60. While his take-off was unspectacular, the half-roll and 180-degree turn with subsequent nosedive caught my attention. He then proceeded flat out down the runway about three feet off the deck. At the end of the runway, he pulled the chopper up hard and fast. Then we leveled out and headed home.

By this time one of my uniforms was in tatters. One leg was torn from crotch to knee; the knee was gone from the other leg. The collar was held by threads. The remaining good uniform was too filthy and smelly to be worn. Given those pitiful conditions, I retrieved a clean Panamanian uniform from one of the barracks. The Panamanian patches were removed and a U.S. flag was sewn on each shoulder. I scrounged deodorant, shaving cream, a razor and some after-shave. At the shoreline I stripped and waded out into the ocean to bathe. It felt good to be clean! My old uniform was washed and hung to dry. I then went for a short walk around the area. It was January 5, 1990; the next day I would be 37 years old.

5 January 1990

2ND OF THE 7TH SFG(A) ARRIVES

I ran into SGM Stone and the two of us went to the airfield to look over the brand new AK-47 bayonets we had found. A line of 2½-ton Army trucks came flying down the runway. The 7th ID, we thought, until we recognized the men in the trucks. On seeing us they slowed to a stop. The battalion CSM, Henry Bone, ran to Stoney and me. He said, "How are you Sergeant John…Hey, that's a Panamanian uniform!" "It sure is," I replied, "and it's the first clean one I've had since before Christmas!" He then turned to Stoney and said, "SGM, don't you need a haircut?" Stoney said, "Yeah I know it, but I've been a little busy lately and had other things on my mind." CSM Bone then asked if we knew any barbers in the area he could hire.

Stoney and I looked at each other then at Bone. We needed to be going, we told him, but would be available if he had any questions. Important questions he should have asked: Were we getting sniped at? What was the public opinion toward us? Were there booby traps or mines still in the area? What was the water status? We did agree on one thing: it was time to pack up and get out of Rio Hato! The place was growing too small!

AIRLIFT TO BATTERY PRATT

This was my birthday but there was no time to celebrate. I was allowed to select six men, one from each team, to accompany me to Battery Pratt. Purely by coincidence one of them had to retrieve his and his friends' clothes from the club in Colon. Attached to the underside of the helicopter that flew us out was a sling-load of booze and souvenirs. The pilot remarked that it was one of the heavier loads he had ever flown; 45 guys can accumulate quite a bit.

One of our final tasks was to find our six rental vehicles that were scattered on both sides of the isthmus. You might know the last one to be found was the Major's, in an American unit motor pool with a suspicious-looking logbook. We had loads of work to get done. The Bat Cave was a mess. Ted Sanders, company supply sergeant, and the rigger who had been unwilling to volunteer for a mission, had been assigned to secure the Bat Cave while we were gone. The rigger did not leave the cave, meanwhile eating and drinking everything he could find, to everyone's disgust. To his credit, he had built fighting positions every 30 or 40 feet the entire length on the inside, with weapons and ammunition at each. The last position was immediately outside the latrine door, perhaps as a means of escape should he need to vacate. Jumping in the toilet and flushing it was a possible escape route.

One day, after many days inside, Sanders wanted to enjoy the afternoon sun. After only a few steps outside the steel door it slammed shut. Some time later a reaction team from Fort Sherman arrived in search of the attackers. Not having seen any attackers, the puzzled Ted asked for an explanation. Base operations had received a report that shots had been fired. The identity of the caller was readily apparent, so Ted started inside to get him. He found the door to be securely locked from the inside; it was much later and after considerable threats of bodily harm on a certain rigger that he could re-enter.

Things soon evolved into chaos. So much had to be done: vehicles to be readied for shipment, tons of stuff to be cleaned and packed, and equipment and nine houses to be turned in. Worst of all was the ammunition, a couple of truckloads of it. Little of it could be accounted for as the guys had brought back what they had found around the countryside. But my luck finally turned—I was allowed a wartime turn-in. I wasted no time in hauling the ammunition for turn-in and clearing the documents. For my own professional well-being, I kept the documents for over 15 years. No way was I going to jail for having done my job; ammunition is a quick way to go there. With only another day left, we were ready to go home.

THE PARTY

The mission was complete, we had no ammunition with which to fight and no radios with which to communicate. Planning material had been properly disposed of, either sent to Fort Clayton or burned. There was only one task remaining: have a party! Base ops on Ft. Sherman was notified of our plan. Any unusual sounds emanating from the hill were to be overlooked. We would phone in the alarm if rescue was desired. The booze was distributed, each man selecting his own bottle. The intensity of our drinking was proportionate to the intensity of the past days and a great time was had by all as we toasted to everyone's safe return and many a good missions.

THE RETURN

Our return home was eagerly anticipated. We had heard stories and had seen telecasts of the 82nd having been welcomed home with much fanfare. We felt entitled to similar treatment, given that 45 men had captured more than 800 prisoners and 3000 weapons, without a single casualty. But ours differed considerably. Pope AFB was secured. The families were not permitted to drive out there but instead were driven by bus. When we did arrive, we endured a formation through several speakers. Then it was General Guest's turn to speak. SSG Louis Vasquez's daughter regained control, though. Having evaded her mother, she rushed pell-mell to the middle of the formation, shouting joyfully, "Daddy! Daddy!" Everyone cheered her on. General Guest, an astute commander, graciously took the hint and abbreviated his speech. He then pinned our CIBs and dismissed us. At the company area we unloaded our equipment and went home.

A NOTE TO FAMILIES

I was home, safe but considerably changed. Life, to me, had become more precious. Sadly, those who meant most to me failed to show how happy they were about my safe return. For several months their continued well-being had been uppermost in my mind. Could they survive without me if I was killed or seriously injured? Little did they realize the strain this had caused me. My concern for them underlay my concern for the mission, the men who served with me and their families. I cannot overstate the importance of a man's family showing their pleasure at his return. Their support enables him to resume a normal life free of the need for preparedness, ready to kill or be killed.

May 23-24, 1990

DINNER IN WASHINGTON

These were two most memorable days. The week before, three of us (Ray Makar, Rick Lazaras and I) had been chosen to attend dinner in Washington, a dinner hosted by Ross Perot for a number of Special Operations soldiers involved in OPERATION JUST CAUSE. We stayed at the Hilton Hotel, just two blocks from the White House, all expenses paid, even the bar tab.

This was a two-part affair. Dinner on the 23rd then a ceremony on the steps of the Senate the morning of the 24th. Dinner was an incomparable experience, attended by many in high profile, including the President. Tables were arranged to accommodate a well-balanced mix of soldiers and prominent civilians or politicians. At my table were Strom Thurmond, Senator of South Carolina; Charles Robb, Senator of Virginia; and his wife Lynda Byrd Johnson Robb, daughter of former President Lyndon Johnson. When introduced to Mrs. Robb, I said, "Dear lady, come here and let me give you a Texan-to- Texan hug!" I don't know which of us was the more surprised. Also at the table were the owner of the Washington Times and a leading Washington campaign consultant. Among those at surrounding tables were the Admiral of the Navy and LT GEN James Grey, Commandant of the Marine Corps. Not least among them were Ross Perot; his son, Ross Jr.; MAJ Dick Meadows (retired SF team leader for the Son Tay rescue attempt); and Lloyd Bentson, Senator of Texas. Ross Jr. was the surprise of the evening. Despite his being a millionaire, he was an F-15 pilot in the Texas Air National Guard. The most important guests were the former POWs.

A TRULY CLASSY LADY

The Washington Times owner introduced Ray, Rick and me to a most interesting person, one of the grand dames of Washington. On shaking hands this grand lady said ironically, "It's so wonderful to be here in Washington tonight. In my over forty years here I've never seen as many real men with real balls in town at the one time." She was the wife of a former Ambassador from Panama and had lived in the U.S. all those years. Our last glimpse of her was when she and Rick made their way to the bar, where they talked and drank most of the night. They were perfectly matched, those two. Had she not been 25 years older than Rick, I'd have bet Rick would not have survived.

MEETING ROSS PEROT

The secretary to Ross Perot had been married to one of my old team leaders, CPT Udo Walters, also a participant in the Son Tay raid. Before meeting Mr. Perot I had asked her if he had a picture of COL Arther

(Bull) Simons, a man I knew he greatly admired, a legend among Special Forces. She said no but thought he'd love to have one. I asked to be introduced. As we shook hands I positioned mine on top then released a 35-mm slide into his. What could I have given him, he wondered, that might interest him. What he found was a photo of Bull giving his last pep talk before launching the Son Tay raid. He said, "Oh my, oh my, oh my! Look here, this is a picture of a real man! My oh my. I gotta go show this." After having shown the photo to several people, he came back, thanked me, and introduced his son, Ross Jr.

A WRONG IS RIGHTED

Before dinner got underway I ran into a Navy SEAL with whom I was acquainted. As we chatted I learned that it was his team that had been ambushed at an airfield; many of them had been severely injured. One Seal in particular was walking with a cane, one hand curled inward. By the shape of his head I guessed that he had sustained a hit there. Now curious, I asked how the young man had been injured. The team had been ambushed by Panamanians armed with a medium machinegun; seven of the team were wounded or killed. This young Seal, their medic, was struck in the leg, wrist and head; he lay on the ground when the shooting stopped, miraculously still conscious. The uninjured team members were helping the others. Based on his assessment of personal wounds he figured he was dying, this sailor refused treatment until the others had first been treated. Being team medic and believing himself to be dying, he directed the others on treatment of the wounded. Not until everyone else had received treatment would he allow personal attention.

On his arrival to Howard AFB his wounds were checked following which he was immediately transferred by medical airlift to Fort Sam Houston, TX. The doctors felt he had less then fifty percent chance of surviving the next 24 hours. His parents were notified and were flown to Texas. Curious about the type of medal he was awarded, I was shocked to find that he had received none. He had been submitted for something but the downgrade resulted in his receiving only a Purple Heart. Back at my table, I ate and thought about the disservice done to him. An idea was taking form. I asked Ross Perot if he planned to speak. With his positive reply, I related this young man's heroism and asked Mr. Perot to mention the young man, if he could. He agreed to do so if I would tell him why. I shared my plan to have the young Seal awarded something more deserving. Now I summoned the courage for the next phase.

The Admiral of the Navy was sitting within arm's reach but I didn't know how to approach him. Seeing LTG Grey in front of me, I had an inspiration. I introduced myself and requested his assistance on the issue at hand. Following my explanation, he wondered why I felt he would bother to help. I informed him that a former aide of his had been my boss for a while. Based on what he had told me I suspected as a fellow combat soldier he would be as mad as I was. What did I want from him, he asked. To introduce me to the Admiral, I replied. Why not introduce myself to the

Admiral as I had to him? Hearing about him from Mike Rapp and reading about him, I was less intimidated by him than by the Admiral. He studied me a moment then led me to the Admiral's table.

As we were approaching the Admiral's table Mr. Perot was citing an example of courage by telling the young man's tale. The Admiral stood up to greet the General and General Grey introduced me. He informed the Admiral that he had a problem and needed to listen. The Admiral beckoned to his aide, who wrote as I told the story given to me. The Admiral ordered his aide to investigate the circumstances in the morning. If it were true, he wanted the situation corrected. Pointing to the SEALS, I informed the aide that he could start immediately if he wanted to. The Admiral looked at him and told him it sounded like a good idea. My effort reportedly resulted in the young man's being awarded the Navy Cross, something I feel very good about.

PRESIDENT BUSH ARRIVES

MAJ Dick Meadows, another Special Forces legend, was speaking when a gentleman walked over and whispered to him. MAJ Meadows leaned forward and asked everyone to stand for the President of the United States. To the tune of "Hail to the Chief" the President strode across the stage. He spoke for 20 minutes; 3 to 4 of those minutes were spent thanking MAJ Meadows for the introduction. The President briefly related Meadows' past accomplishments and his recent return from a mission. The President stated that Meadows would probably soon be going out again. That provocative remark stirred some curiosity from the Times editor, who began to ask me some probing questions. When the presidential speech had ended, at the first opportunity I spoke to Meadows. Knowing that he wanted to discuss a joint mission for later that year, I apprised him of the Times editor's persistent questioning. We agreed to table the talk for a later date.

A SMALL PRIVATE PARTY

The speeches concluded, the room was abuzz with conversation. I joined three SEALs, as did Ross Perot Jr. The five of us moved to the lobby drinking and talking until after 3 o'clock that morning, when each went to his room. The following morning would be filled with activity.

24 May 1990

DAY TWO

After a breakfast buffet we were taken by bus to the Senate Building. On the steps several Congressmen spoke: first Robert Dole, future presidential candidate, and last Richard Gephart, Senate majority leader. While Mr. Gephart was speaking, I moved to the rear of the sitting area, hoping to stay awake; I had slept little the night before. Senator Dole joined me and we made casual conversation. If Senator Gephart was the best the Democrats could offer, I quipped, the Republicans were sure winners. What did I mean, he questioned. Senator Gephart has been has been giving a campaign speech for the last 10 minutes, I responded. If he

91

thinks these soldiers are interested in listening to his self-aggrandizing speech, he did not understand his audience. Hasn't anyone told him that he lost his party's nomination to run for President last year? Senator Dole laughed uproariously, nearly tripping over a chair.

Senator Gephart must have noticed our enjoyment because when he finished his speech, he began to approach us. On seeing him close in, I said apologetically to Senator Dole, "Oh heck, here he comes! With all due respect sir, I'm going to move away. I don't even want to shake his hand! I'm afraid I'm going to have to leave you to deal with him." I went over and had further conversation with Mr. Perot and thanked him sincerely for everything he had done for us. That done, we departed for the airport for the trip back to Fort Bragg. Senator Gephart was soon to justify my feelings about him. Just before Desert Storm, he stood on those same steps of the senate, threatening to introduce legislation that would curtail funding to re-supply the troops if we moved toward Baghdad. What kind of a man would threaten to cut off the supply of food, fuel and bullets to soldiers of his country engaged in combat just to prove a political point? With the mixed signals some politicians were sending it was no wonder we had to fight in DESERT STORM.

Above: Me and SFC Arroyo standing at Fort San Lorenzo, Panama Nov 89
Below: Outside the entrance to Battery Pratt on Fort Sherman Panama. We lived inside it for 2 ½ months.

Right to Left: Colonel Gonzo Gonzales, President
Fidel Castro and three unknown. Picture is at Rio
Hato, Panama in Aug 89. (Photo of a photo)
Below: Two men in the center are Colonel Gonzo
Gonzales on the left and Ramon Castro on the right.
Rio Hato, Panama, Aug 89 (Photo of a photo)

Above: Me on a MH-60 Blackhawk on my way to David, Panama, Dec 89. My M-24 sniper rifle is just behind my right elbow.

Below: Pecora River Bridge looking North from near the position of A/3/7th SFG(A) on 20 Dec 89.

Top: The civilian airfield at Santiago, Panama. A/1/7 captured this first then called the garrison at the bottom and it became the first to surrender under the "MA BELL" concept Both photos were taken in Jan 1990.

Above: MAJ Richard (Dick) Meadows introduces President George Bush at the Patrick Henry Dinner in Washington DC April 1990.
Below: Senator Bob Doyle and myself on the steps of the Senate the next day.

June was spent wrapping up preparations for a six-month mission building a 900-man Peruvian training center in the middle of enemy territory for the Peruvian Army. The mission was ultimately canceled for reasons that will remain unknown.

A new team sergeant was assigned, Bob Cuadra, giving me the opportunity attend some schools. His being a MSG and my being an SFC meant he was Team Sergeant. After language school I attended a few weeks of sniper training. We also began to prepare for a trip scheduled the week after I finished training.

October 1990

COSTA RICA

We were in country on 7 Oct, arriving at the San Jose International Airport and moving directly to the National Police Academy in the suburb of San Antonio. The six-week course was much preferable to Saudi Arabia. Forty students from different law enforcement agencies in Costa Rica were to train in counter narcotics tactics; the English title for the course was "Advanced Anti-Drug Tactics." For the most part training proceeded smoothly. We built a shoot house and that training ended without incident. Training included recon techniques, ambushes, OPORDs, patrolling, basic and advanced shooting techniques, and room clearing. To the north of Punta Arinas map reading, land navigation and additional patrol practice was conducted.

FOOTBALL DE COMBATE

Physical Training (PT) with the students was challenging for both participants and spectators. Two days of the week were spent playing "football de combate" or combat football. The rules were fairly basic. Anyone who approached the ball or appeared to approach the ball, regardless of distance, was liable to be tackled, knocked down, or run over. What took place was a combination of karate, judo, wrestling, football, soccer, and hand-to-hand combat. The more senior members of the team selected half the student class and the junior members the other half. Nicknames were given: I was "the Ancient One," Ski was "Robo Cop," and Shawn McNabe, who wore size 15EEE shoes, was "Big Foot." Several nicknames I've since forgotten. Markers were used to write the names on T-shirts. The academy soccer field was our arena. The game was rough; it was not unusual for a player to seek out the medic during or after the game.

There was considerable taunting between our students and regular academy students. Our guys would tell the other class that they weren't playing a tough man's game and the other class made comments back. The challenge got thrown out one day and the other class accepted. Word was spread of the showdown to be fought one week later. Even the school commander was drawn in. He announced that after lunch next Friday there would be a training holiday. Families were to be bussed in, refreshments sold, and the game filmed. It was to be a major sporting event.

Wednesday morning we played the final split class game. The National Minister of Health happened by. He observed the game as the commander detailed Friday afternoon's game plan. As he watched, four players were carried to the infirmary. That was too much for him. The commander was told that future football de combate was forbidden. So the Friday game was canceled. Had we played, the game of soccer in Costa Rica might have been forever changed.

THE GORGE

Behind the academy lay a very deep gorge, more than 200 meters/600 feet deep. Weekends were free so one Saturday several of the guys decided to rappel to the river at the bottom of the gorge. Bobby McCaig, Jim Tunstill and Dave (Ski) Tomaleski wanted to go down. They ask me to come along; at first I declined. However, knowing that none had experience with long rope descents, I reconsidered and told Bob Cuadra perhaps I should go. Dang! It took almost three hours to reach bottom. Why? The ropes were only 120 feet long. Good anchor points for the ropes were difficult to find. And a site had to be carefully selected where everyone could get off the rope without falling to the bottom. At times there would be a man on one small ledge and two on another. I would be on a third tying off another anchor point.

The last pitch down was rough for Bobby McCaig. Ski and Jim had already gone down. Bobby and I were on a ledge about 3 feet long and jutted outward only 18 inches from the face of the cliff. Bobby faced the rock, a cigarette in his mouth. He hugged the cliff face so tightly the cigarette broke off at the filter and pointed upward toward his eye, filling his eye with smoke. That eye was tearing and Bobby was saying, "Ron, I think this ledge is too small for two of us. Let me go down next, OK?" I passed the rope around me and let Bobby hook in. He stepped off and headed downward slightly fast. As he passed through the top of a 70- to 80-foot tall tree, his foot was caught in the fork of a branch. He turned upside down and got wedged in the tree. Bobby was in a mess and we were powerless to help. After ten minutes of struggle, he freed his foot and he rappelled to the bottom, where Jim and Ski were watching.

We scouted for a path up or down river but none was to be found. Crossing was not a viable option; this was a class 6 or 7 river, no one would be able to cross. Our only course of action was to select a route and start back up. Everyone agreed that I should lead. We headed back on the easiest route up I could find because the others lacked experience climbing. There was also the rotten make-up of the wall we were climbing. I would move up and find a place to position myself so the others could use the rope for assistance up the cliff wall. At one point a rock came loose and struck Ski on his back. Fortunately he was carrying a pack with a radio in it. The rock struck the case, and caved it in, but Ski was OK. About four hours later we neared the top and so took a welcome break. Across the gorge was a crowd of 60 or more had gathered to watch us from the top of that side. An enterprising man was selling refreshments from a cart.

By now we were only 20 feet from the top but there were problems. It was an overhang, we carried no technical gear, and it was getting dark! In desperation I briefly considered tying everyone off and waiting until someone from the team came to look for us. Another rope could then be dropped to us. To add to our difficulties, rain appeared imminent. And when it rains here it's usually a downpour. I didn't relish being miserably wet and cold all night. Then I spotted a small tree hanging over the edge just a short distance away. The tree didn't look real sturdy but I hoped it would work.

The guys were positioned so they could move over if I made it up. A quick lesson on belaying was given to Jim Tunstall, who, I fervently hoped, would do fine. One end of the looped rope was thrown up. I climbed up first, the rest followed. On top we collapsed to the ground. This could well be the only time I ever saw Ski exhausted. But my appointed belayer, having become nervous about the task, had untied the rope from around his waist while I was climbing. Never again would he belay me!

The 200 meter deep gorge we rappelled into.

HALLOWEEN 1990

The Costa Ricans thought that Halloween was a significant holiday to us who were away from home. To ease our sorrow, they planned a surprise; no one on the team had a clue. Shortly after 9:00 p.m. the door flew open and in marched a horde of Halloween creatures: a mummy, a Ninja Turtle, a pregnant bride, and a witch and her little animals. Each of us was gifted with a coffee mug and small bag of candy. The creatures were a sight to behold. The mummy was encased in at least 4 rolls of toilet paper. The pregnant bride could push his stomach out until he really did seem pregnant, the mustache only enhanced his looks.

November 1990

PUNTA ARINAS

San Antonio was not sufficiently large to conduct an effective land navigation course so we went to Punta Arinas. The ranch on which we lived and trained was owned by the first cousin of President Calderon of Costa Rica. Don Victor Lobo who is a most interesting gentleman. His ranch was large, 20 square kilometers. The quarters were somewhat crowded but the place was suitable. It came with a cook, which helped a great deal.

One night a student came running in with news that another had been bitten by a scorpion. It was a minor injury, which the medic quickly treated. The injured student had been arm wrestling with another student; he lost the contest when his hand was forced down to the scorpion on his side of the table. Future contests were prohibited. In a couple of weeks we returned to San Antonio.

GRADUATION

Based on the number of VIPs attending the graduation, the course must have been thought important. Among the VIPs were a fellow from the U.S. Embassy, the Minister of Justice, and the national chief of police. And Don Victor Lobo. Maria, the woman who had seen to our needs while there, was tearful when presented with a small gift. She was the witch on Halloween. I presented her a sketch I had drawn; she displayed it in her living room wall, I heard later. It was time to go home.

November 1990

THE AIRPORT

At the airport, surrounded by our equipment, we were told by one of the Embassy staff inspection would be conducted by Costa Rican customs agents. We anticipated a delay of considerable magnitude. The inspectors arrived, calling out to several of us. It was two of our students. They asked if we could find our football, which we retrieved from the pallet. One of them took off running and Ski threw him a pass. We were soon running and passing the football until the C-130 showed up. There were spectators watching through the airplane windows, probably wondering who we were.

THE FLIGHT HOME

Until midpoint on our return flight to the US, the trip was uneventful. Then the aircraft crew chief was busily running around looking worried. Apparently the AC wouldn't hold air pressure due to a small opening up near the nose of the aircraft. After a brief discussion we offered a sleeping bag, which he tried and it worked. When he emerged from the small passage after stuffing the bag in the hole we had our chutes laid out just in case we needed them. With that we continued to Pope AFB.

December 1990
NEW MEXICO
We had been home for ten days when Chief Bush and I were off to New Mexico and Cannon AFB to prepare for team training scheduled for the first of the year. That was it for 1990.

Feb-Apr 1991
THE TOUGHEST TRAINING, EVER!
I was in the most challenging training offered by Special Forces, nicknamed the Mental Ranger Course, 12 seven-day weeks and 16+ hour days. The volume of writing was such that the end result was callused finger tips on the writing hand. The use of computers or typewriters was not permitted; everything was handwritten. In one four-day period I had slept a mere four hours. Thankfully someone else would drive back from where we were training; there was no way I could have. The rigorous schedule meant relaxed grooming standards which lead to the following humorous stories.

For the final phase I had left the house a well-attired professional, clad in a three-piece suit and carrying a briefcase and was a marked contrast to the returning graduate, clad in blue jeans, a brown Carhart coat, a flannel shirt and brown civilian boots. When that phase was finished my hair halfway covered my ears and I had grown a beard. A neighbor almost called the police on seeing me enter the house upon my return. When I went into the company I went past the operations office and MSG More ran out of the office and called out "Hey sir, civilians aren't allowed back there without approval." I turned around and ask him "Moe, are you talking to me?" He couldn't believe it was me.

Another amusing tale from this course occurred on the return flight. Here we were, wet, cold and hungry, as usual waiting on the AC. The plane landed in an open field about 2:00 in the morning. We streamed out of the darkness and boarded the plane. With barely room for all, we managed but for one, a warrant officer, who was forced to sit in the co-pilot's seat. Chief was excited; it was the first time he had ever sat up front. After take-off he shared with the pilot his excitement and his secret longing to fly some day. Jim, the pilot, instructed Chief to place his hands on the wheel and his feet on the pedals, after which he briefly explained the gauges and the azimuth that needed to be maintained. Jim then told him to keep it steady he was going to take a nap that Chief was in charge and in an hour was to awaken the him, Jim then pretended to sleep.

On nearing Pope AFB, an excited Chief awoke me to ask if I thought that was Pope AFB coming up. I said I thought so and advised him to awaken Jim, who I knew was listening because he chuckled to himself. Acting as if he were coming out of deep sleep, Jim resumed the controls. He then radioed Pope Ops and requested clearance to land. His request was denied; landing was only for military AC. Jim radioed back with his tail number, urging a speedy computer check as he was on final approach. With that he rolled the plane over and went into a steep descent. There was loud commotion where our plane had been directed to park. They thought they had a bunch of VIP's on account what came back on the tail number check. There stood an 18-year-old Air Police (AP) with his M-16. Instead of the VIPs he had anticipated, departing the airplane were long-haired men in civilian clothes, several with beards, and all carrying AK-47s. That young AP looked at us and decided he best secure his M-16 back in his truck. His officer was eagerly awaiting the VIPs on board. We neglected to tell him it was a training operation but instead unloaded our gear into unmarked vans. The officer continued to wait for the pilot to climb out but we told him that a one-legged, one-eyed fat man could not be expected to climb down just to get fuel. We continued loading up and left him waiting.

May 1991
NEW TEAM SERGEANT FOR ODA 713

In my absence MSG Pat Dillion was appointed the new team sergeant. His tenure was not amicable, to say the least, and was disastrous for the team. Within one month every senior team member had requested a transfer. By the time I finished the course, the senior and junior weapons, senior engineer, and senior medic had already asked to be reassigned. When I tried to discuss the situation, he rudely informed me that he would speak with me when he needed to. If he didn't discuss it with me, I warned him, I'd transfer out as well. He'd already destroyed what Bob Cuadra and I had built. He didn't want to talk so I was reassigned to Battalion S3 shop the next day.

May 1991
THE BATTALION S3 SHOP
Working in an S3 Operation Section can be a great experience with the right staff. Initially I worked with MSG Paul Dowdy, which was not the first time he and I had worked together at this level. Both of us believed we could make a difference. With subsequent personnel changes, however, conditions began to deteriorate I felt. To make matters worse Paul put his retirement papers in and retired.

June 1991
JRTC AND FORT SILL, OKLAHOMA
When I had been back two weeks the entire battalion of 1st of the 7th deployed to the Joint Readiness Training Center (JRTC). We were based at Fort Sill, Oklahoma and inserting teams into Fort Chaffee, Arkansas. The procedures ran smoothly. I had developed a system for tracking message traffic to and from the teams that aided us greatly. We were the first battalion to have tracked 100% of the message traffic at JRTC. While there I celebrated 20 years of military service. Drinking a couple of beers with SFC

Russell who also was celebrating 20 years that month was the extent of my celebration.

A NEW WAY TO RESUPPLY

The desire to leave behind something to be used by Special Forces was one of the reasons for my returning to an Army career. Here was the opportunity. Special Forces and Military Intelligence teams in the field were in desperate need of resupply. The opposing forces (OPFOR) had located and placed under observation every potential drop zone (DZ) and landing zone (LZ) within the operational area. If a chopper attempted a resupply he would likely get shot down, and that usually happened when it was tried. The system I developed worked off the FAST rope bar on Task Force 160 choppers. Several hundred pounds could be put through an opening in the trees as small as 10-feet in diameter when needed. The choppers could settle into the treetops for the necessary 5 or 6 seconds, positioned so that shooting was possible only from a higher hilltop or directly below. LTC Lambert, the battalion commander, loved it. This system was used about a dozen times without one chopper being shot down.

I had discussed the concept with SFC Ray Makar. I had also drawn it on paper and described the function and testing. Ray put it together and we started testing the next morning. When all was readied, we went together to the test site which was off the top of some bleachers under a tree. After some minor tweaking we tried it then demonstrated the process to the commander. He approved it and that night the first two resupply operations were conducted.

The commander was quickly convinced that this process needed to be demonstrated throughout Special Forces. The Task Force 160 commander also liked it. LTC Lambert believed that a film would sufficiently impress the SF Command CG to support development. We made the film and back at Fort Bragg I submitted it to Joe Alderman at the Special Warfare Center and School (SWCS). Unfortunately he became ill and died before development could be completed.

October 1991

The Master Sergeant list was to be out soon and several guys asked if I was to be on the list. I had no inkling; ironically I was totally unconcerned. Many others were wondering about it for themselves.

November 1991

The list was finally distributed. The day before its release a SGM friend of mine told me I was on it, sequence #1. My disbelief was overcome by much effort on his part. The following morning I hunted down the list; my name was listed as sequence #1. That meant I would be the first promoted from the list and would be senior all others promoted from the same list. There was the added financial benefit of a $300 monthly pay raise. It's hard for many to understand that I wasn't extremely excited like others. One must understand that SF may send numerous SFC's or lower ranked sergeants on a mission but will only send one

MSG generally. Now my ability to get on certain missions was narrowed by promotion.

1 March 1992
PANAMA REVISITED
This morning, at 0600 hours, I departed for Cabanas 92. We were apparently to advise 20th SFG(A) on running an intermediate support base (ISB) in Panama. We were primarily to conduct resupply and recovery operations for teams that would infill from Honduras. Once more Battery Pratt was our base of operations, as it had been for 2½ months before Just Cause. Not much had changed inside. There were things we had left behind, such as a building model we had built for planning. There was a flood of memories, as they say.

IT'S A SHARK
From the operational standpoint, it was business as usual. What free time we had was spent on memorable activity. There was the afternoon when a team member and I went snorkeling by the Fort Sherman gate. There was a large hole in a coral reef, which I was certain, sheltered a lobster or two. Taking a deep breath, I pulled myself down by the coral and peered inside. Two black beady eyes were looking back at me. On the surface I called to my fellow diver to look at the big fish. After a brief moment he surfaced and exclaimed excitedly that it was a shark! Laughingly I agreed. I told him I wanted to kill it if I could. My spear gun was cocked on the back notch to deliver maximum power. My companion was armed with a sling of mine, fixed with three 10-inch barbs.

With him on one side and I on the other, down we went. Rather than coming out of the hole after I shot it, the shark retreated farther back into the hole. I pulled and pulled until the spear came out, along with a baseball-sized chunk of meat. He and I surfaced, I again cocked the spear gun, and down we went. This time when I shot the shark, it thrashed about a moment then exited out. As it did so, my companion speared it with the sling. The two of us managed to get that three-foot long shark to the surface and to the shore. In retrospect we decided that our action had been foolhardy. We were in some of the most shark infested water in the world and we did not know how large a shark we were shooting. We speculated on what we would have done had other sharks showed up or if this shark had really been large. Any way it made enough to add to a fish fry later. With the possibility that other sharks in the area would be attracted by the injury to the first, we left there and went to Hidden Beach.

SURPRISE ON HIDDEN BEACH

There were some funny moments at Hidden Beach, the first occurring as we approached the beach one afternoon. One of the guys from 3/7th SFG had apparently told his wife that no one ever came during the week and she was persuaded to sunbathe in the nude. The path to the beach was through 100 yards of jungle, so no one could be heard driving up. At least that couple did not hear us. As we walked out onto the beach she saw us, screaming as she jumped up. Her discomfort at having to simultaneously cover her breasts and genitalia, meanwhile giving her husband devil, was quite hilarious. Giving up the attempt at modesty, she donned the suit bottom first. Being the gentleman that we were, we turned our backs while she dressed. Afterward we all had a good laugh, but she swore that never again would he be able to persuade her to sunbathe.

TUG OF WAR WITH AN OCTOPUS

Later I was snorkeling and noticed a small cloud of silt outside an 8- to 10-inch hole. Once more I was convinced I had found another lobster. To be on the safe side I advanced the spear, tip first. What a surprise to have a 3-foot long tentacle came out and wrap around the spear shaft. We battled for the spear, me pulling out and he pulling in. We alternated pulling a few moments. I gave serious thought to shooting it, but octopus meat is not my favorite fare. Besides, this was the first I had ever seen in here. A problem soon developed: my air supply was running out. Remembering the sharp point on the end, I guessed that by poking the octopus, he would release the spear. Again we pulled. Suddenly I pushed rather than pulled and succeeded in poking him. That was enough for him, he turned loose and I surfaced for air. I chuckled at the thought of what I would have thought if it had attached himself to my facemask as I peered into the hole What a sight that would have been as I shot out of the water.

42 Ks OF WHAT!

On one of the last days we were there I found a young sergeant from 20th SFG lying on his bunk. Because this was his first trip out of country and he had been too busy to look around, I advised him to take someone with him and go down the trail in back of the battery to the beach and explore the area. He thought that was a good idea and went to recruit a fellow explorer. Meanwhile I had to go to Fort Davis. On my return from Fort Davis a couple of hours later the young sergeant excitedly informed me of his find. Thinking that he had found a dugout canoe or something similar, I asked what he had found. Forty-two kilos of pot on the beach! Stunned, I asked him again. To convince me he took me to the beach. Pot was certainly what he had found! I sent for the CID to retrieve the stash. Evidently some smugglers had thrown it overboard and it lazily drifted to the beach.

1 April 1992

MASTER SERGEANT

Today I was promoted to Master Sergeant. When it was time to change rank Josie, with great enthusiasm, ripped the old one off and with real gusto and threw it over her shoulder into the crowd, to their amusement and laughter. This promotion was important in that I could be transferred from the S-3 shop and resume a team sergeant role. Within a week I was assigned to Company B, 1st Battalion.

ODA 721

I was assigned to ODA-721, which did not have a team sergeant. Team members were CPT Preston Short (team leader); SFC Frank Suarez (intel sgt); SSG Bob Horrigan (senior weapons); SGT Mike Olague (junior weapons); SFC Steve Wilshire (senior engr); SSG Antonio Burgess (junior engr); SSG Chuck Hayes (senior medic); SSG Doug Garrett (senior commo). I was team sergeant. My new team had a mix of some very capable members and some not so capable. One man was pending possible discharge from the Army as a result of an incident more than a year before. Suarez, Wilshire and Horrigan were the more senior men I had. Olague, despite his looming problems, would do well with guidance. Before our scheduled deployment in one month, I had some work ahead of me. (I'm happy to say SSG Olague did well and managed to retire later.)

May 1992
HONDURAS, HERE WE COME, AGAIN

On the 15th we deployed to Honduras, landing at JTF-B/Soto Cano in the afternoon. There was little time in which to draw ammunition and vehicles for departure the next morning, our destination was the Honduran 2nd Battalion in Tamera. SFC Steve Shirly was the new medic who accompanied us in place of SSG Hayes, who was in language school. The next morning we left for the battalion at Tamera, an airborne school and their only airborne unit besides their special forces. The trip would be brief, only 3½ weeks, but our plans were intense. We ran a light infantry course for a company not long out of basic training. The course ran smoothly and all went well. The course included training in medical, communications, marksmanship, movement, recon, patrolling, ambushes, raids, mortars, machineguns, land navigation, basic demolitions and airmobile operations.

The final exercise was impressive and exciting. One of the country's four generals had come to observe and was very pleased. He and the battalion commander, COL Jose Perria, claimed that we had accomplished more in three weeks than the previous unit, nearly a full battalion, had in six. The first exercise was a company helicopter infil. The entire company, once on the ground, moved out in patrol order. At a selected point the support element broke off and moved to a position up on Point Diablo from which they would provide fire support. The rest moved to the attack position. At a signal from the attack position the support troops opened fire on targets with M-60 machineguns and 60-mm mortars. With the second signal they shifted fire to the left and we moved forward with the attack force, setting off 18 different explosive charges as the students advanced to add realism to the scene. The target secured, the attack forces placed their charges and blew it up as they withdrew. It was a heck of a show! To wrap things up we conducted a joint airborne operation, after which we exchanged jump wings. After many delays, we departed for home.

September 1992
INTERNATIONAL PARACHUTE COMPETITION
The team went to Rhode Island to participate in the International Military Parachute Competition. Wind and rain, however, allowed little of the planned events and not one of the many international teams could jump. There was one very interesting story, though. A party was planned for Saturday night. The

instigator who provoked a drinking competition among the senior NCOs remains a mystery but the honor of the US team was at stake. I was obligated to defend that honor in competition with the German, Canadian and British Senior NCOs. The contest raged for a couple of hours then the Canadian stood up and asked me to slap him. I judiciously declined and continued to do so but the Brit joined in and encouraged me to do it. In the interest of international sportsmanship, I finally agreed but warned the Canadian that I planned to lay it on him lest he thought me a woosey. At his insistence, I advised him to get ready; he said he was. I slapped him with a force that caused his eyeballs to roll in the orbits, or so it appeared. I really didn't want to do this, but?

He looked at me glassy-eyed and demanded to know why I slapped him. I nervously replied to this hulking gorilla that he had insisted on my doing so. He denied it but fortunately for me the Brit and German supported my claim. Momentarily disoriented, the Canadian commented "that it was a bloody stupid thing for me to do". He finally reckoned that he owed me his commando T-shirt, which I exchanged with my Special Forces T-shirt.

ODA 722

The company SGM asked me to take another team, ODA-722. This was a dream assignment for me: this was a mountain team. Why would I want to change to another team? Climbing was a passion for me. The present team leader of 721 was someone who failed to heed the advice of more experienced members. The company commander had twice asked if the team leader should be fired. Covering the team leader's backside was a time-consuming job. And the two of my best team members had just came down on assignment orders. For those reasons, I felt it was a good time to leave, given the opportunity. ODA-722, here I come! My first task was to provide the team some mountain training, which no one had. In fact, none had ever been on the rocks at all. My team members were WO2 John Hodge (team tech and commander); SFC Bob Opsitnick (intel sgt); SFC Oscar Santiago (senior weapons sgt); SSG Robert Torres (junior weapons sgt); SFC John Barnard (senior engr sgt); SSG Jamie Jauregi (junior engr sgt); SSG Mike Halterman (senior medic); SFC Mike Rios (senior commo sgt); SSG Fred Widner (junior commo sgt). Once again I was team sergeant.

October 1992
THE VIETNAM MEMORIAL

On October 2nd the team left Fort Bragg for Mountain Warfare School at Jericho, Vermont. En route we stopped by the Vietnam Memorial. Vietnam was a war in which we all knew someone, perhaps even a relative, who had been there and who may have died there. I myself found the name of someone with whom I had grown up. Kenneth Shamblin and I had attended grade school, junior high and senior high together. We had played all the sports together had shared many other activities. He was someone well liked. To my knowledge, he never even had a fight while he was growing up. I found his name at the center left, near the top. He had served two tours as a door gunner and crew chief and had been shot down more than a dozen times. He had survived all until the last, when as he climbed out of the wreckage, a sniper shot and killed him. I was living in Atlanta, Georgia, when I learned of his death. At the funeral I grew to despise the hippie, dope-smoking punks and the draft dodgers shown on TV.

SUMMER MOUNTAIN WARFARE SCHOOL

Mountain Warfare School was some of the best training ever; the team agreed. The instructors excelled in something they'd been doing for years. Most considered it not only a job but also a hobby. I was pleased with my personal performance. One of the most challenging climb routes was aptly named Ice Cream. Anyone who succeeded in this very difficult climb was treated by the instructors to a pint of Ben and Jerry's Ice Cream. Of the entire class, I was the first to succeed on it; only two others did so. Of those two, one was a team member and the other a Canadian Mounty.

SAVE ME!

As always there was a humorous incident to be shared during this training. The first days were spent climbing sheer verticals. The instructor would climb beside the trainee using ascenders on a rope and coaching the trainee along. The climber would be top roped so that an accidental fall would be limited to a few feet at most. As SFC Oscar Santiago was climbing, he fell. On reaching the end of the rope he became a human pendulum swinging toward the instructor. As Oscar came into contact with the instructor, he screamed, "Save me!" then held on with his arms and legs wrapped around him. As a result, the instructor began to yell for someone to get Oscar off him. The class of spectators found this immensely hilarious. One team member advised the instructor to make sure he still had his billfold. Oscar finally turned him loose and resumed climbing. The entire team did quite well. Bob Opsitnick finished first, I was fifth; four team members were among the top 10 in the class. I was gratified that I had done well: I was 40 years old and in 1979 had been told by a pair of Doctors, I might never walk again.

November 1992
THE BLADEN COUNTY DEATH MARCH

The team completed the most grueling event anyone over 40 could imagine. I had pushed myself beyond my own expectations, at least since having sustained severe trauma several years before. First was the 12-mile march, each member bearing 55 pounds in a rucksack, plus water, weapon and helmet. The march I finished in 2 hours and 20 minutes. Immediately after everyone had come in, we were loaded in the back of a truck and were driven 25 miles in temperatures ranging from the high 30s to the low 40s. We arrived at our destination, cramped and stiff from the ride. We then chuted up for a combat equipment jump following a 25-minute plane ride. On jumping I was still stiff from the ride so I was painfully jolted when the chute opened. Even worse, on landing excruciating pain shot throughout my body. I lay on the ground, gingerly moving one body part at a time to check for any fractures. The intensity of the pain brought tears to my eyes. When I had determined that nothing was broken., I rolled over onto my stomach, rocked back on my knees, crawled to my ruck, which I then used for stabilization as I stood up. Despite the pain coursing throughout, I managed to remove my chute and roll it up. I could barely carry my equipment to the turn-in point.

From there we went to the range to fire our rifles and pistols. Then we boarded the helicopters for Bladen County, an area notable for its swamps and thickets. On the ground we had to march 10k to our first point where we had to write a complete battalion OPORD in Spanish before moving on. This took about two hours. Our next point was 10k away and here we had a brief wait for instructions. We proceeded to the next point 14k away and en route were ambushed. According to the controller, we had three wounded. So in the dark we started IVs and wrapped bandages. Then we were instructed to move the three wounded and their equipment to an exfil point 2k away. The six of us, each carrying a ruck weighing on the average of 60 pounds, carried our three wounded and their rucks. To make the task even more challenging, we had only 30 minutes in which to do this; yet again we made it in time.

At the exfil point, where the three injured were miraculously healed, we were then given five 40-pound catering charges and four cases of chow to carry on our next 18-k leg. Of course there was a time limit for this task as well. Halfway to our destination, we came to a small river. I directed a recon to the left and right to find a crossing point, but no luck. We were thoroughly exhausted. At this point, falling into the cold water could prove to be fatal. So we built a big fire around which we gathered and took a much-needed break. The men were concerned that CPT Boyles would show up and make us start over. I assured them that if the captain or SFC Eckert showed up and said anything, I would personally throw them in the ice cold water. This would of course discourage them from staying too long and bothering us! Within two minutes everyone was asleep. Fred Widner was snoring so loud the animals couldn't sleep.

It was daylight in two hours, so we moved out again. The jump had left me stiff and hurting. We walked until we found a place to cross without getting soaked. Around 10:00 we reached our destination. And here we had to prepare a platoon OPORD in Spanish at the same time conducting weapons, demo and ambush training. Several hours later we moved out with the troops we had been training and conducted an ambush. After moving about 2k away, we split off and headed for our next point. It was still daylight so we found a spot and rested until dark. Somehow we were slightly ahead of schedule.

At the next position a human rights abuse was being simulated. Our task was to stop the abuse and evacuate the injured individual. We were given a victim on a stretcher: a 7-foot railroad tie with an oak 2 x 6 nailed on each side. We immediately headed for the exfil point but after 100 yards we came upon another river. John Barnard stripped down, swam across and anchored a rope. The rope bridge system was used to get our victim, ourselves and our equipment across, all somehow remaining dry. We quickly gathered our equipment and headed out, switching off every few hundred yards. At last we made it the 6k where the victim was dropped off. At this point we were given two hours to get to the team exfil point, 12k away through some of the worst countryside in Bladen County. After checking the map, we took off. We had been alerted to watch for SFC Eckert. We were told he was taking sadistic pleasure in declaring that those he found had violated a rule, necessitating their return to the last point and starting over. This would naturally cause delay so that the team would miss the exfil time and would have to walk another 15-20k to the alternate site. We resolved not to miss our point. Moving toward our destination we heard Eckert driving up and down the road, stopping once in a while and calling to us to come out of the woods. We quietly out-waited him, losing time doing so. To make up the time, we moved to a road and started moving at a jog. The noise of a vehicle would send us scampering into the woods or swamp to hide. I had suffered partial hearing loss, but my ears soon became attuned to the unique sound of Eckert's truck, which I would be the first to hear. The first couple of times I shouted for the team to get off the road because I could hear the truck, the team was unbelieving knowing my hearing loss; after two times they obeyed without hesitation.

At one point we walked along a trail through the swamp, each man would tell of his fatigue and hunger, of steaks, shrimp, potatoes and all kinds of food, and of crawling into a big soft bed to sleep when this was over. When it was my turn, I declared that I would settle for a bowl of corn flakes and a cot, where I would sleep undisturbed for 24 hours. The guys thought this was hilarious. I had forgotten this story until I was in Panama in 1997and Jamie Jauregi laughingly reminded me.

We arrived at the exfil point with two minutes to spare. The chopper was coming so we took off running to set up the landing zone and quickly signal with IR strobe lights. As the chopper landed, I directed the men to load. As we scrambled into the chopper, we heard a pickup truck. We shouted at the pilot to take off, meanwhile pulling the last two men in on each side. We were sure it was Eckert. Sure enough he pulled up and climbed out waving us back. Those of us in the door saluted him with our middle-finger victory sign and screamed to the pilot to keep going. We landed on a small LZ on Fort Bragg and were ordered to await the trucks that were to pick us up later in the day. The worst now over, we could hardly care. We ate quickly then climbed into our sleeping bags to rest. In 48 hours we had walked more than 70 kilometers and had carried loads that at times weighed more than 130 pounds. Also the temperature never rose beyond the low 30s at night. All we asked for was time to sleep until we were transported to the battalion area.

We had to be awakened by the transport team, who patiently waited for us to pack. We were all eager to get in and head home. The driver then reluctantly informed us that we were to be debriefed by CPT Boyles. No one wanted to listen to a debriefing delivered by someone whose experience was limited to his having been a chopper pilot for 10 years and who had served only 10 months on a team. I shared my strategy with Jauregi. We would listen to CPT Boyles but if he got long-winded, I would signal to Jauregi. He was then to announce a trip to the latrine, going instead to the front office to call the team room. I would answer the phone and pretend that CPT Boyles was required elsewhere; and we would escape the moment he left. As we had expected, CPT Boyles' debriefing was interminably long, so the signal had to be given. As CPT Boyles walked out one end of the building, we ran out the other. We never did finish that debrief.

December 1992
HEARING AIDS
By the Army's standards, my hearing had severely deteriorated. Hearing aids were deemed necessary and I was to obtain these at Walter Reed Hospital in Washington DC. It was a bitter pill to swallow, although I'd suspected it for some time. As often happens, something good can come out of something unpleasant. At Walter Reed I called my former company commander, MAJ Ed Phillips. He was at this time liaison officer between Special Operations and the Drug Enforcement Agency, with his office located in the White House. I invited him to dinner. He declined but insisted that I come at 1900 hours the next night to the west wing entrance of the

White House. That next evening at 1900 hours, 1 Dec 97, I entered from 17th and G Street. After the guard had entered my name into the computer, I was given a pass and allowed through the metal detector down the hall. Thank goodness Ed showed up about then because I'm confident that I'd have lost my way. There were several locks to be opened before we could enter. For an hour we talked of old friends and times past, then he said we were going on a tour of the West Wing.

I was then taken on a personal tour through the halls of power; the most interesting of all were the communications center and War Room. Introductions were made then we snaked through the equipment to the War Room. I had imagined it to be much larger; in reality it was small, measuring 20 by 15 feet. The reason for its smallness, Ed explained, was to limit entry to only key people. Next to the War Room was the conference room, similar in size, but with several TV screens for video teleconferencing at the far wall opposite the presidential seat. The highlight of the tour was my sitting in the big chair in the War Room. It was only for about 5 seconds but sitting there meant a great deal. From that chair men had directed the history of nations. Fairly heady stuff for a country boy, and something for which I cannot thank Ed Phillips enough.

January 1993
A CITIZENSHIP OBTAINED
One problem had been nagging at us: SSG Jauregi's citizenship status. When his father brought

him to the US from Cuba, no citizenship papers were submitted. He could not apply for a passport therefore and his time was growing short. The law dictated that one could serve in the military for six years without a U.S. citizenship; Jauregi had served more than five. What were we to do? The Battalion and Group, who themselves could do nothing, gave me free rein to accomplish whatever I could. I called the top lawyer for the Department of Immigration in Washington, DC. After several phone calls we finally spoke by phone. Given the peculiar circumstances and the need for Jauregi to accompany the team, the lawyer agreed to help. I was given the private telephone number for the head of the Immigration office in Atlanta, Georgia and I was to inform her that he had given me her number. She was only too happy to help when she found out who had directed me to call. She asked several questions then said she would mail by overnight express the forms Jamie needed to complete. Meanwhile Jamie had called his father to send the necessary documents. Everything was assembled within 24 hours and sent to Atlanta by overnight mail.

The woman called and said everything was in order; Jamie was to be in her office in three days for the swearing in ceremony. This was helpful but he still needed a passport before he could leave with us. The only solution was to have him drive straight from Atlanta to Washington DC as soon as he got sworn in. We called the passport office and were told that since most of the papers were available, we would be accommodated. And that's how SSG Jamie Jauregi received his citizenship and passport in less than ten days.

ECUADOR

This next section differs from the rest because it represents a daily log of the trip. So much was happening that to distinguish the trip from the other sections of this book, I chose to leave it this way.

5 February 93. We left Fort Bragg for Latacunga, Ecuador where, for the next six weeks, we will live and train with the 9th Special Forces Brigade Mountain School at their camp north of town. This is also home for the Paratrooper School. ODA-732 will join us, as will two lead climber instructors from Vermont. The first four weeks will be spent at the Ecuadorian Mountain School followed by two weeks of lead climber training, and finally joint training and an airborne operation. The camp is very scenic. A tall statue of a paratrooper, surrounded by a wall of fallen hero's, stands guard at the entrance. The chow is pretty good, too. The only problem is water. All drinking water must be bought bottled water or water we bring from the embassy in Quito, a distance of 120 k.

6 February 93. Four of us are going to survey a drop zone for future use. Lack of air is quite noticeable when moving about. Shortness of breath is a common problem with exercise or work. Lethargy wraps you like a blanket, making it very difficult to awaken. We've been given Diamox to take for the

first few days. This drug is meant to enhance the blood's ability to absorb oxygen.

8 February 93. I haven't written in the past couple days because the last 32-36 hours have been miserable. I've probably gone to the latrine 20 times; the rest of the time I've been in my bunk. I know I'm severely dehydrated so I'll ask the medic to administer an IV. I hope this is my last day in this dreadful state.

We had a guest instructor today, Christian Munchmeyer (P.O. Box 17-12-0770, Quito, Ecuador). He taught us Andean history, ice climbing techniques, and altitude sickness. He taught from personal experience, having climbed on all seven continents with some of the world's best. He taught in the morning and we taught knot tying in the afternoon. We knew the knots but we didn't know their Spanish names.

9 February 93. This morning we all went for an 8k ruck march; at this altitude it was a butt kicker. At 1100 hours we had PT. Doc skipped the physical part because of his broken toe.

10 February 93. Today we did a 10k/6mile ruck march for starters and then conducted rappelling and communications classes the remainder of the day.

11 February 93. No hard PT today because we have a long ruck march tomorrow. Today we did rope bridges, equipment familiarization and issue. I also called home this evening.

12 February 93. Started the day off with a 21k ruck march, slightly more than 12 miles. Our team outperformed the other team. We finished ahead by as much as a half-hour on the average. The finish was at a 100-foot-tall railroad bridge where we did some rappelling. A number of townspeople were our spectators. There must have been 60 kids watching. Along the way I took some beautiful pictures of the mountains and a 400-year-old aqueduct. Thank goodness there was a truck for the way back. But this was the month of carnival, part of which includes wetting people with water. As we rode through Laticunga a lady atop a building threw a pot of water, wetting some of the soldiers in the truck. Everyone laughed about it and the lady waved.

WATER BALLOON AMBUSH

13-14 February 93. The weekend is here. Saturday was spent checking out Laticunga. On Sunday we moved to Quito, home of the 1st Zone, 13th Brigade. From here we will be launching to do a few climbs this coming week. En route to Quito we drove through a fairly large town where we spotted two guys with water balloons. Jamie ducked back just in time, a water balloon barely missing him. Believing himself to be safe, he stuck his head out just as the third guy nailed him. It was all in good fun. At a restaurant I had just stepped to the counter to order lunch when two fine-looking young ladies walked by. The guy behind the counter excused himself, reached under the counter, grabbed two water balloons and hurried outside. Calling to the girls, he hurled one of the balloons. He managed to get both of them wet, making his way back to applause from the appreciative crowd.

15 February 93. We went out to a bridge that spanned a deep gorge for ascender work off a point where it was 100-foot or more from the ground up. That was that for the morning. That afternoon I toured the downtown area of Quito and bought leather jackets for Josie, Darius and me.

16 February 93. We climbed some this morning but the rain made it impossible for the afternoon. I had bruised my heel jumping from one rock to another; so an afternoon of rest won't hurt. SSG John Barnard and the two lead-climber instructors from Vermont (CPT Eckleston and SP4 Kontos) were directed to look for a lead-climbing training site. While awaiting my turn, I sketched a monastery at the bottom of a mountain and some of the rocks on which we were climbing.

17 February 93. Today we would climb our first big mountain, one of the two Volcano Pinchinchi. This is a 15,000-foot peak. On the way there we realized it wasn't the best day to climb. There were several low-lying clouds and the temperature was very cool. As the Army truck lumbered up the mountain and into the clouds we ran into some rain, which made the steep winding road even more dangerous by making it extremely slick. On these roads a truck could slide down 1500 feet or more before stopping. Much of the way there visibility was limited to less

than 25 yards in front but we drove until the trucks could go no farther. We then continued on foot. The rain-slicked surface did little to deter us; we were determined to make this one. But the higher we climbed, the more it rained, and the wetter we got. We were coming to snow-covered ground so it was even colder than where we had started. An overhang gave us a much-needed shelter out of the weather and underneath we took a 15- to 20-minute break. At this point we were one hour from the top and about 14,000 feet up.

Once on our way again we noticed that there was now sleet mixed with the rain that pelted us at a 30-degree angle. The terrain was such that anyone who fell would not require attention from the medic. I wondered how much farther we could go without proper equipment. At last CPT Abondo halted us and asked if we wanted to continue. Will the weather continue to worsen or break, I asked. Worse before it gets any better, he replied. We voted unanimously to start back down while we still could.

Everyone was wet and cold so no one complained about turning back. Only when the clouds broke momentarily did we realize how high we'd climbed. Getting back to the trucks also took longer than anyone had thought. In the trucks heading down the mountain, it became apparent that the excitement had just begun. As close as he could manage, the driver hugged the banks to avoid slipping over the side, scraping paint off the sides of the truck in doing so. With each turn we moved as one to the up-hill side of the truck. And just in case, we kept one leg positioned to jump. We survived the harrowing ride back to town. Tomorrow we will try the other Volcano Pinchinchi.

18 February 03. Success today, we made it up the other Pinchinchi. Getting up to the launch point was very interesting, to put it mildly. At first it looked as though the rain would once again hamper our efforts, but our luck held. As we crossed over a mountain and looked down, and I do mean down, the sun came out of hiding and shone on one of the most beautiful valleys to be found anywhere. Sheep and cattle were grazing on the greenest grass imaginable. The small and very clean community was lined with cobblestone streets. The valley seemed to be in another country. With the turns on the mountain so steep, the driver often had to reverse and climb three or four times to negotiate the turn. It was a replay of the previous day, with us stopping several times to get out, throw mountain grass under the tires and push the truck to keep it going.

On reaching the launch site, we climbed out of the truck, donned our packs, and made our way up! But for the thinness of the air, it wasn't a tough climb. On top were a couple of reminders that any mountain can kill. Two plaques were mounted on rocks, the first to a German who had died a couple of years before and the other to a Canadian girl of the month before. We took a few photos and started down. Our luck had run out; rain was starting to fall again, ruining any chance to take good photos. Back at Quito we loaded up and headed back to Latacunga.

19 February 93. Not much happening today. Most of the guys went shopping. John Barnard remained and he and I checked and cleaned our climbing gear.

20 February 93. The camp commander came with the Colonel who headed all the paratroopers in the country. They asked if we would participate in helicopter rappelling and STABO demonstration in the town of Imbato. No one was at US MILGRP who could authorize this so I decided we would, based on who had asked. I called and left a message for the MILGRP commander then John and I grabbed our gear and went with the Ecuadorians. We stopped at the camp near Imbato and planned our demonstration with the Ecuadorian soldiers. We would rappel from a French Puma helicopter 140 feet up. Because of this, and for safety reasons, we would use our gear. A CPT and I would be the first two out, one on each side. John and one of their sergeants would follow, invert, and descend upside down. We rigged the bird and took off. From high above I saw more than 50,000 people seated in the soccer stadium. While the chopper hovered, I threw out my rope and watched as the end landed on the ground. I gave the signal and the CPT and I dropped out each side. Underneath I signaled to him to go then I cut loose, free-falling and watching the ground rushing upward. I braked as the belay man on the ground belayed me. I had braked so hard that he was thrown into the air, landing on his

face.   Quickly backing off the rope, I photographed John as he came out and down.

John and his partner exited the chopper, dropped about 15 feet, inverted and caught the rope between their feet, and descended. It was spectacular and the crowd was impressed. On the ground two more soldiers ran out as we tied figure-eight knots in the end of the ropes and two more ropes were dropped. When everything was ready the four were hooked on and they STABO'd out. Soaring over the crowd, John dropped several handfuls of candy. The crowd roared, with kids running here and there after the candy. What a great movie that would have made, if only I had brought a movie camera.

We were in the middle of carnival week. Later we viewed all the displays at the fairgrounds. The commander invited us to watch the parade downtown. He assigned a couple of bodyguards to John and me, so we changed into civilian clothes before heading downtown. The parade was festive and colorful, with several hundred fine-looking senoritas dancing down the street and beauty queens riding the floats. I was taking pictures when Jorge, my bodyguard, persuaded me to go out in the street for better photos.   A policeman ordered us back to the side. Jorge flashed his ID and the cop quickly moved on. After he had done this several times, I asked Jorge about his official status. Apparently he was a member of a special group with special authority, even over regular police.

STREET DANCING

A funny thing happened during this parade. The parade stopped while a group danced in front of us. With the dance over, I persuaded one of the dancers to allow a close-up. I had just snapped the photo when the band started up. The dancers ran to the crowd grabbing at partners. A young lady grabbed me and I soon found myself dancing the salsa in the middle of the street. Jorge was laughing at me when her girlfriend grabbed him and pulled him out into the middle of the street. My face was probably as red as a firetruck but it was all in good fun. The crowd was entertained by my surprised and embarrassed look. After four hours the parade was over. Jorge, John and I caught a bus back to Latacunga and a taxi back to camp.

22 February 93, Monday. Today we did a 15k hike at about 12,000 feet in Cotipoxi National Park. I missed having my camera because the day was perfect and Cotipoxi was magnificent. Next week we will attempt to climb it to the top. This will be a serious climb of six hours, starting from 15,000 feet to 20,000 feet. It is the second highest peak in the country.

23 February 93, Tuesday. Today we did land navigation in the mountains. It started at 12,000 feet and would have an 800-to 1200-foot difference in altitude between points on each leg of the course. Talk about a butt-kicker. Pass the O2 please.

EVACUATING A WOUNDED SOLDIER

24 February 93, Wednesday. Today was a good day for our team but not so for other team. The weather was ideal when we started up the mountains for a day of weapons-firing. From the parking location we began the two-hour walk up the mountain, our backs laden with weapons and targets. After 30 minutes SSG Barnard became sick so I sent him back to the parking area to rest. For the past 12 hours he had suffered from a stomach virus that had stricken the team, one man after another. At 2000 feet up from our starting point, or 14,000 feet, we stopped; the other team began to set up their range. I questioned the wisdom of their site, uphill from us, which could prove to be a hazard. Arguing was pointless. The other team sergeant was senior to me and his captain supported his decision to proclaim themselves in charge of the range. Chief and I held our team back from participation. I told SFC Torres to fire our explosives rounds downhill, not uphill.

After the first volley the other team moved, still firing 5.56- and 40-mm HE, their targets no farther than 100 meters uphill. With the degree of risk this presented, I felt obligated to share my concern with the other team sergeant. Although they had finished firing, I did so. He was annoyed but that was of little concern to me. I returned to Chief, who related that a soldier from the host nation had been wounded in the leg by 40-mm shrapnel. Having been told by Doc the severity of the injury, I informed the other team leader and team sergeant of the situation. We had to shut down, I urged them, and get the victim off the mountain. But after they had discussed the situation with Doc, they chose to continue firing.

Chief and I were angered by their apparent lack of concern. The injured soldier's wound was in the upper leg. Assessing for internal hemorrhage was difficult to do in the present circumstances. To add to the difficulty, the trip down the mountain would take an hour, and another hour to reach the doctor at battalion. They could not be persuaded and were not the least bit concerned. Chief and I presented the situation to the soldier's commander then asked for six men to help us. Cpt. Abondo agreed. Torres and Juariga were instructed to do our firing down the hillside; the rest of us would move the injured man down to the vehicles. I was damned proud of our team, who made the rope litter then, with assistance of the host nation soldiers, carried the injured soldier from above 14,000 feet to 12,000 in just under an hour. Two men sustained minor injuries on the way down but to this day I can picture our bringing the guy down, switching out every 200 yards or so. I sent Doc to accompany the man to the hospital.

Thoroughly exhausted after that ordeal, we all lay down and fell asleep. While we slept the weather had took a turn for the worse. On our awakening, it was snowing and sleeting on us. There were two inches of snow by the time the other team got down the mountain. Then the 2½-ton truck had to be pushed by hand before it would start. Halfway down the mountain the weather cleared and we felt a little less miserable.

In gratitude for our compassionate deed, CPL Nelson Reyes made a mountain flute for us, which he presented to each before we left a few weeks later. The night of the accident, we went to the house to check on him. We must've been introduced to all who lived in that end of town, and many of them plied us with drink. My head was hurting come morning.

GENERAL BUENO RESCUED

Still stewing over the other team's lack of concern about the situation, my team chose to ride, exposed, in the back of the truck. It was a miserable ride. We were slowing down. Curious, I looked up over the top and saw up ahead a terrible traffic accident. The truck stopped as a young lieutenant ran breathlessly alongside, exclaiming his general was in the car and needed assistance. This was a serious wreck. The front end of the car was gone and the engine had been thrown about 50 or 60 feet. I told Jauregi to check the general while the others were organized to flag traffic and conduct crowd control. I walked to the car where the general lay, complaining of his back. Jauregi and I crawled into the wreck to place the general on our small backboard and apply a collar around his neck. The others then assisted in extracting the general from the car. We had planned to use the other team's rental vehicle to transport the general to the nearby military hospital. However, the lieutenant informed us that this was the General of Intelligence for the country and could be transported only to the military hospital in Quito, 120K away. I then ask him what he would do if I decided to instead take the general to a closer military hospital? The Lt. then informed me he would have to shoot the General! Well, we sure didn't want the Lt. to do that so we loaded the general into the rental vehicle and away they went. Jauregi accompanied the general, as did Cpt. Abondo.

En route Jauregi was preparing an IV when the General protested. Jamie said, "Sir, right now I'm the closest to a doctor you have. If I feel you need this, then you're going to get it because right now as the medic I'm in charge." The general received the IV; it probably prevented his going into shock. On hearing Jauregi speaking to the general the way he had, Cpt. Abondo himself nearly required medical attention. Jauregi was later vindicated when the doctors approved of the attention given the general by the Americans, which may have saved his life and almost certainly had prevented his becoming paralyzed.

Back at Fort Bragg a few weeks later there was a letter from Gonzalo Bueno, General of Intelligence for Ecuador, thanking us for our services. The letter had come through State Department channels and so meant quite a lot to the team. This had turned out to be a heck of a day for the team. Our actions had earned us the respect of the Ecuadorian military, whose subsequent interaction with us differed markedly with that of the other team.

THE MOUNTAIN RUMIAWA

25 February 93. Big day today; we did a 17,000-foot climb. We left the launch point at 0830

and walked about 7k uphill to reach a point 5000 feet above where we had started. The climb, while not difficult, was extremely dangerous. This mountain was in fact an old volcano, with the ground not at all solid. Often, it seemed, you would look at a protruding rock which would suddenly loosen and fall. For the most part the slopes to our right and left were 75 degrees to sheer verticals. The temperature wasn't too bad at this altitude and the wind was calm today. The Ecuadorians had failed to brief us properly for this climb and there were not enough lines to enable everyone to tie off properly. Barnard and I used my 7-mm line, 70 feet long, leaving enough ropes for the others. Occasionally someone up ahead would dislodge a rock and would call out "roca" (rock). I would flatten against the rock face and listen. Tinkle, tinkle was a little problem. Ker-thump! Ker-thump! Now that was a big problem. This sound heralded the descent of a large rock; there was little you could do but flatten yourself and pray it did not land on you or someone else.

John and I were in a chute when we heard the distinctive thump, thump of a large rock coming down. We simultaneously dove into a crack, shouting "rock!" as we dove. No sooner had we jammed into the crack when the rock bounced immediately above us and came past us brushing John's backpack. We shouted "rock!" again as it made its way down, bouncing off the sides of the chute in which we were tightly jammed. Then came a completely different sound. After another thump or two, the sound again differed. I shouted down to the others, asking them their status.

Two of our men were struck by the rock. SSG Mike Halterman, our medic, was hit on the back but his aid bag had absorbed most of the blow and he was unhurt. SFC Bob Torres was not so lucky. The glancing blow to his helmet had left him somewhat stunned. Mike was the first to check on him. I dropped down to where they were. The two of them were fine and were joking about the incident, but we all realized we had been lucky. A rock of that size can knock a man off the mountainside and his partner with him. Farther up another rock came loose and again Doc's aid bag saved him from serious injury.

The worsening weather did not deter us; we were too near the top. Our path was often obscured by the clouds and at times our visibility limited to 20 yards. Sooner or later we would reach the top, weather permitting, and we were determined to make it. Those who wanted to turn back were allowed to. Of the two teams only 9 of the 20 Americans who had started up the mountain now remained. We started up again, refusing to give up. We made it to the top—John Barnard, Robert Torres, Mike Halterman, Jamie Jauregi, me, four guys from the other team, and three Ecuadorians. We stayed only 10 minutes because it had begun to sleet very heavily. The weather prompted Cpt. Abondo to lead us down a faster route. It was 1330 in the afternoon and time was a critical issue now because we had to be off the mountain before dark. Without sufficient suitable gear, it would be impossible to spend the night safely in that high altitude.

We reached at a point where a rope could be tied off and from which Cpt Abondo thought we could short cut down at and then Cpt Abondo rappelled down. At the end of that 160-foot rope he called out and asked to be pulled up; this was not the correct location. He was lucky because this was a spot from where several of us could pull him back up. He now knew where he was; we had to climb back up a short distance and traverse over to the correct point. So up and over we went. This time it was the correct site. We climbed down to a point where we rigged again and took another long rappel down. It had stopped sleeting by now so we could proceed more quickly. At many locations throughout we would hastily rappel down and move on. When the clouds broke, we rested briefly. The valley below was transformed by the clouds into a hazy, surreal fantasy. This time, when we moved forward, I brought up the rear with SGT Jorge Santana. Some members from the other team seemed to me a bit clumsy footed. I didn't want to be in the way if something was kicked off or one of them fell and tried to take me with him. We leaped 20 feet at a time and slid down the last thousand feet, through some of the finest spree imaginable. By 1700 hours we were back at the trucks.

26 February 93. Today we taught the first of the classes we are to teach. The Ecuadorians must've thought they were good. They asked if we would be running a course for them while we were in country.

27-28 February 93. In Quito this weekend we stayed at the Hotel Colon, one of the finest in the country. And for a change, I was by myself. In this peaceful and relaxed setting I wrote in my journal, ordered in and watched TV on Saturday. Sunday morning I got up and ordered in and took another long, hot shower. Later that morning I went to the main park to shop among the artisan booths scattered throughout the park. Many handmade items could be found there—paintings, jewelry, wood carvings, leather goods and the like.

1 Mar 93. We moved to the mountain Cotipoxi, our home for the next week, 15,000 feet or 4860 meters up. From there we would train and prepare for the climb to the peak at nearly 20,000 feet. Our shelter was a refuge constructed by the government to house climbers who intended to climb the peak. On the downside we had to carry all our food and water 1000 feet farther than the highest point reached by truck. On the second trip, this time carrying water, I walked with four Frenchmen who were also climbing that week. At the refuge was gathered a multinational group. Besides the French there were three Germans accompanied by an Austrian female, Americans (us), Ecuadorians and an Argentine gentleman, 35 of us for the moment living together. Strangest of all in this adventure were the sleeping arrangement. The bunks were bolted together in a pyramid, four in the center, three on each side, and two on the outside. If you can picture that, now add another set of bunks similarly stacked and bolted to one end. That structure was the main sleeping area,

with two other rooms in which three or four people could lie on the floor in their sleeping gear.

2 March 93. Ice climbing, self-arrest methods and crevasse rescue procedures were reviewed today. We had a very short distance to travel—out the back door 50 feet or so to the foot of the ice field. Training was accelerated by necessity; at midnight on Wednesday we would ascend. This left us very little time. Weather was another factor; good weather was needed for training. A storm would drive us into the refuge where we would await its passage. During this training period we sent radio messages to Panama to update them of our daily status. What did they think of our transmitting from and living at 15,000 feet? Few people realize that on the taller mountains the final push often begins in the dark of night. Fewer avalanches happen after midnight and this is when the snow bridges have solidified as much as they will. It is a race to reach the top just at daybreak, snap photos, and rush back down to the base by noon before the snow and ice turn more dangerous.

3 March 93. At 1300 hours today were returned indoors where Doc gave his final class on high altitude illnesses. Panama also alerted us to the fact that on Thursday the Commanding General of US Army South, MG Timmons, would arrive to verify our daily reports.

0100 hours 4 March 1993. We stepped out the back door of the refuge for our climb upward, wearing headlamps and crampons. The weather was initially calm although severe winds would meet us on the way up. It was easy that first hour; after the first thirty minutes we stopped long enough to secure ourselves, three men to a rope, for safety. Just in time because not long after that a step forward dropped me through a snow bridge as I moved across a crevasse. In that instant, knowing what had happened, I spread my arms out and caught just under the arms. Very carefully and gingerly I tried to feel the walls with my feet, without success. The team immediately did what they were supposed to and came to my rescue. After getting out I crawled back to the edge and shined my light down but could not see bottom because about 30 feet down it curved back out of sight.

After a while it was increasingly difficult to breathe with each step, just as we had read in stories of climbing. The higher we climbed, the harder the wind blew and the colder it got. At 3:30 my headlamp batteries gave out. So to the bill of my cap I clipped my AA-powered mini-mag flashlight. And for as long as it worked, it did so fairly well but 45 minutes later the flashlight also gave out. Luckily I could easily make out the shapes of the men in front and could see their lights. The sky was also beginning to lighten. I was glad, too, that we were near the top because I was developing high altitude intoxication. If my condition worsened, I would have to get back down quickly so that I would not present a danger to the others. I intensified my concentration and even drank some water, knowing that the cause was most often dehydration. Each step was excruciating; after 20 steps or so the three of us would stop to breathe. The excitement at seeing the top helped us forget our agony. Almost at the top I realized that I was too intoxicated to continue up. I told Jamie Jauregi and Mike Rios to help me down quickly before the disorientation worsened.

I fell twice on the way down. The first time I waved as I slid past the other two then realized that I had better self arrest. Twenty feet from where I stopped was another crevasse. I suggested to the other two that we shorten the lines between us or take up some of the slack by putting more space between us. What I had learned from the training I would remember only fleetingly. We safely reached the refuge, where I took some aspirin to fight the monster headache, got an IV, drank lots of water, ate some and after a few hours sleep had fully recovered.

Still more climbers came this afternoon, two Germans, two Dutch, and two Argentine. To end the day we planned a small demonstration for LTG Timmons for tomorrow morning, where the vehicles were parked.

THE BRIEFING

5 March 93, 0815 hours. We moved down, laden with equipment, and 100 foot above the parking area we set up our display. When questioned why we hadn't moved closer, I replied that the General should personally experience the breathing difficulty up here. They laughed, knowing that coming from sea level even 100 foot uphill would take the wind out of the General. The display was nicely presented. On the

first poncho lay the cold weather equipment we used and the clothing we wore. On the second and third ponchos lay rock and ice climbing equipment. On the fourth poncho were the medical equipment and a rope litter we had constructed. Then we waited. Coming across the valley was a convoy of rental vehicles bearing the General and his travel group. I gave the men the one-hour warning; by my reckoning it would take that long for the general to drive 2000+ feet up the side of the mountain. My estimate was almost exact. Chief Hodge and I greeted the visitors at the parking lot. With the General were the US MILGRP commander and an Ecuadorian general, and seven others.

We invited the group to the display site for our briefing. I purposely walked rather quickly and on arriving asked the General if he was ready. He requested a few moments to catch his breath. How, he asked, did we endure this rarified atmosphere? For the past month, I told him, we hadn't gone below 10,000 feet. He stood at 14,000. How high did we intend to climb, he asked. We had lived 15,000 up for the past week, had climbed to 20,000 feet the day before, and after a couple of days down at 10,000 we would move to a site 16,000 up, where we would stay for four days in the upcoming week. The General was suitably impressed.

For the briefing each man stood behind a group of equipment, briefing the group and answering their questions; the system worked well. After John's briefing on the climbing gear, the General commented favorably on the Army's having provided improvment with more modern equipment. I cleared my throat and explained to him that $2000 worth of that equipment was owned by the team members and that much of the other had been borrowed from the National Guard in Vermont. Was there any way he could help, he asked. I explained to him that a letter from him would go far in better equipment being funded, we all chorused.

What most interested him was our working relationship with the Ecuadorians. The MILGRP commander reported on some joint activities and I filled him, relating things I felt were relevant. At the conclusion he presented each of us a USARSO coin because, he said, we were some of the best Special Forces soldiers he had ever seen. He assured us that once back in Panama he would let others know of our outstanding accomplishments. With our visitors off the mountain, we loaded the trucks and headed back to 9th Brigade's camp for some well-deserved rest.

6 March 93. Graduation for the Andanista course was held today. The speakers done with, the certificates were presented. ODA 732 presented to the Battalion a small plaque they had bought, a replica of the 7th SF Group coin about 18 inches in diameter. To the commanders they gave a bottle of Bacardi rum. But there was one last gift for the school—a 4 x 4-ft knot board we had constructed at Fort Bragg. On the board were mounted all the climbing knots labeled both in English and Spanish, and several pitons as well. The school commanders and their instructors were impressed by our gift, which was later mounted

in the entrance to the building. On a brass plate was engraved "From ODA 722 To Our Brothers of the Mountains, 1993".

THE PARTY

Later in the afternoon we celebrated on the camp grounds, with good food in abundance. Afterward two large trays with mugs were brought out. Each beer-filled mug had in the bottom an Ecuadorian Special Forces coin. One by one, we were each called forward to make a toast, then everyone would down a beer. The toaster was to catch the coin between his teeth as he drank the last of his beer. The next man would come forward while the mugs were refilled, then the toast made. Not to be outdone, I collected everyone's 7th Special Forces Group coin. Then I then called each Ecuadorian forward, one man at a time, to imitate our toast, each mug filled with beer and a 7th SF Group coin. The beer was gone by the last three toasts, so we switched to rum; this was our undoing. We reeled back to the barracks, to be overcome by alcohol-induced sleep.

7 March 93. After Chief Hodge's two-hour computer class, the other team was transported to their drop-off point from where they moved up to the site for lead climber training. That move and our return to camp consumed the rest of the day.

8 March 03. The team went to the rifle range today where I taught them bullet trajectory. There was noticeable improvement in their marksmanship from the last time. From the starting point at 15 yards, we

moved back in 25-yard increments until we reached a 275-yard distance. With plenty of ammunition available, the pace was unhurried and the aim more deliberate and steady. Not only were skills improved that day, but self-confidence as well.

9 March 93. Computer training and nothing else all day.

10 March 93. The morning was spent in weapons class to include the Styr Aug SG-77, 9mm Uzi, Mauser 8mm, 9mm BHP, S&W model 59 and the MAG 58 medium machinegun. The afternoon was spent retrieving the other team from the mountain, made necessary by bad weather. Our team goes up in the morning.

A BULL IN THE ROAD

11 March 1993: We left as planned at 0800 and the two-hour trip was very pleasant. While driving through a mountain pasture 12,000 feet up, we came upon a bull standing proudly in the middle of the trail. This magnificent animal glared at us interlopers, his front feet spread, ready to charge, guarding his departing herd. Pride and defiance were his special mark. Curious about the blue silk ribbon tied around his neck, I asked one of the Ecuadorians about it. He stated the ribbon symbolized victory for this veteran of the bullfighting ring. Satisfied that his herd was safe, at last he allowed us passage.

When the trucks could go no farther, we unloaded for the hour walk up the side of the mountain to the campsite 16,000 feet, on the southern side of Illiniza South. The site was set up, we ate, then made ready for the trek to the training site around noon. Our efforts were blessed by unusually good weather.

12 March 93. Another great training day in clear weather. Late that afternoon, though, Doc said that SP4 Kontos, was suffering from HAPES sickness, and had to be taken down a bit. This altitude sickness can kill a man if he isn't soon taken down from the high altitude. He was helped down the mountain, loaded on the truck whereby I drove him down to camp for a few days of reset and recovery. It was late when I returned, exhausted by the day.

A BIG WEATHER CHANGE

13 March 93: I awoke the next morning to the sound of a freight train coming through the camp. I struggled out of the sleeping bag but soon realized that the three-man dome tent was down on me. Still in the sleeping bag, I maneuvered until my head was near the entrance, which I unzipped to look outside. A storm passing through had dumped an inch of snow on the ground the storm clouds blanketed the camp. There was nothing to be seen beyond 25 yards. I shouted to Chief Hodge, suggesting that we give it another hour or so and attempt to wait out the weather; he agreed.

The weather was here to stay for a while, so we broke camp. Breaking camp was the easy part; moving our gear from the training site 800 foot above was the hard part. Barnard, Jauregi, Echelston and I went to remove the equipment from the cracks in the cliff face. We had stored it there to avoid having to climb with it every morning. The danger lay in retrieving the anchor points from the cliff tops. My first load down, I started back to help with the rest. About halfway there I met John and the Cpt. Jamie was just a few minutes behind them so I thought I could help him a little. Had I not seen his shadow, I would've missed him walking through the fog. At the campsite we assembled our equipment and headed down to the vehicle. There was only the Suzuki Samurai truck into which all the equipment was loaded, and one man with equipment piled on his lap. The rest went on foot as I drove on the slick mountain trail. Most of the men beat us to the lower regions. The truck unloaded, I drove back up and picked up the men as I found them.

14 March 93. Today was spent cleaning equipment and hanging it to dry.

15 March 93. Chief Hodge and a few others went to survey another climb site while the rest of us turned in school equipment and packed non-essentials. That done, some of us went for a haircut. No other suitable climbing site was found so we chose to go to Quito in the morning. This proved to be a problem because we had only one vehicle. The other team had two but they were busy goofing off. Our strategy was to have three men ride the bus tonight and stay at the hotel Colon. In the morning we would shuttle the rest back and forth the short distance.

16 March. Frustrated by the other team, I lost my temper with both the team sergeant and team leader. Our equipment allowed little room in the truck. One man still had to remain behind so I chose to stay. A second vehicle could not be borrowed from the other team, They wanted both of trucks available should they decide to go somewhere. I was angry at their crappy treatment after my team had done so much to cover their deficiencies. Not only had they wounded a host nation soldier, they did nothing to support the idea after having announced to everyone that there was going to be a party. Every weekend my team had gotten water and when they asked, we assisted them with our vehicle. Hell would freeze over before their team ever goes with my team anywhere again.

17 March 93. The men stayed in town again last night so they could have another day of lead climbing. This would give the team eight qualified lead climbers, more than any other team in 7th or 3rd SFG. As for me, I went to the range with my 9-mm pistol and M-16 and plenty of ammunition and spent the day shooting with three of the Ecuadorian battalion shooting team members. Who was the better shot was unimportant; we were four serious shooters that day. I fired 150 rounds of 9-mm and 560 rounds of 5.56-mm. The men were coming in from Quito when I got back. They also had word that tomorrow's jump was a go.

SALINAS, ECUADOR

18 March 93. At 0700 we left for the airfield; at 0900 we got word the plane would be late. Some of us went back to camp to get civilian clothes for a night

in Salinas. The plane arrived at 1230 and we were airborne by 1300. There were about 20 Americans and a dozen Ecuadorians aboard an old Buffalo aircraft flying through the Andean Mountains. At one point in the flight I stood and looked out the window. I swear I saw a Sheppard's hut about 40-50 yards off the tip of the wing on the side of the mountain. With that I returned to my seat and buckled up.

Lady Luck smiled on us this afternoon and we were able to get in two jumps. Overnight lodging was officer housing on the naval base. As a team we ate and had a few drinks with the Ecuadorians. Someone had provided a bottle and a couple of the men got a little drunk and turned in early. There were some throbbing heads the next morning for our final jump.

TWO INJURIES
19 March 93. Our jump was uneventful but I can't say the same for another team. Two of their jumpers, in an argument over right of way, had become entangled while descending. Nearing the ground they shoved away from each other, thereby landing hard, each sustaining severe back injury. SSG Halterman, our team medic, and another medic, SSG Patch worked on the injured two. How unfortunate that these injuries would probably result in both men leaving the military when they had recovered somewhat. The episode prohibited more jumping for the rest of that day so we headed to the airfield to await word on our return to Latacunga. At 1400 both men were ready for transport. They were carefully loaded on the airplane. Our first stop was Quito, where we were met by the

MILGRP commander and an American doctor. The injured men were checked then sent to the hospital.

We continued to Latacunga and that night ate dinner at the Officer's Club, where we exchanged jump wings with the Ecuadorians. This solemn and old Airborne ceremony was done by each man giving the other blood wings. That is, the keepers are removed from the back and the wings are positioned against the other man's chest then the 3/8 inch pins are driven in with a quick punch. We all retired early, anticipating a full day.

20 March 93. The whole day was spent on the demo range, where we trained and fired the last of the demo we had brought. Around 1300 Chief Hodge left for Quito to make final arrangements. That night we finished our cleaning and packing; we load out in the morning.

21 March 93. We were loaded and on the road by 0800. At the Quito airfield we quickly loaded the airplane and left for town, our last night in country. I ate dinner in my room and reviewed paper work. Then I dressed and went to Le Car, the club where the team celebrated a great mission. Back at the hotel I played the slots for three hours, my total winnings, 2000 sucres (US $1.10).

22 March. Once again we were at the airfield by 0700 and ready to go. CPT Abondo came to bid us farewell and to wish us luck in the future. The MILGRP commander, noting the stronger bond

between the Ecuadorians and my team, asked me why? Whatever reason I gave him must've been satisfactory but what I really wanted to say was that the Ecuadorians knew the other team lacked leadership and dependability. At 0830 we flew out for Panama where we would spend the night. Two of the men, SFC Torres and SFC Opsitnick, will leave at 1000 hours on a second bird and link up with us in Panama. There was one flaw in our link-up plan. The C-141 carrying our two men broke down in Esmeralda, EC, and was delayed four days.

23 March. We're North Carolina bound this morning, with only two stops for other men and equipment. El Salvador and Guatemala were the two stops. In Guatemala the plane broke down and our afternoon was spent baking on the runway while the plane was repaired. We were in Fort Bragg by midnight.

A NEW BATTALION COMMANDER

1 April 1993: Payday formation was interesting. Our new battalion commander, LTC Remo Butler, stood in front and asked for ODA 722. I raised my hand and called out a reply. He stated he hadn't yet met us but planned to and that he had yet to hear of a team performing a mission so well; whatever we were doing the others needed to find out. Proof of our outstanding performance lay on his desk—over ½ dozen letters praising our last mission. The letters were quite interesting and had come from many: the US ambassador to Ecuador; LTG Timmons, USARSO Commander; LTG Bueno, General of Intelligence for

159

Ecuador; US MILGRP Commander in Ecuador; the Commanding Generals for USSOC, USASOC and SF Command; U.S. MILGRP Commander, Peru; Commander of the Ecuadorian Mountain School. These letters cited six different topics and would prove to be useful in the team's getting things in the future. The few months of Red/Support cycle meant no missions for a while, and some of the men attended school. The Chief and I went to JRTC for a month's work with 20th SFG at Fort Polk. With another mission upcoming, planning will be done as time allows.

September 1993

BOLIVIA

Off to Bolivia to teach an anti-narcotics course to the UMOPAR in Chimore, (pronounced Chimorae). The UMOPAR is a semi-secret police force in the country. What distinguished it from other units in South America was membership by high school graduates, at a minimum. Chimore is in the heart of the Chapare region, generally thought to be the heart of the Bolivian drug country. It lies only 120k south of the town where Butch Cassidy and the Sundance Kid were shot a hundred years ago. Fact is, it's still a wild town.

The fact that we were training was to be kept secret but it required approval by their congress. So of course we were met at the airport in Santa Cruz by CNN; some secret. We were driven to an estate that had been confiscated from a drug lord. We stayed that day but were taken to a hotel for the night before leaving on the 120-k drive to Chimore. The following morning, before the mission was to have started, one man was nearly removed from the team. I play by the Big Boy rules. Never allow the mission to be affected by your playing and never play harder than you work. The almost nonmember had chosen to sleep in with his hangover and had even hung up when I called his room. His poor decision nearly resulted in his being ordered to board the first plane home. Two of the men were sent to his room with a message that he was to be downstairs immediately or he would be left behind. His drinking was limited for the rest of the mission. I felt his resentment at the penalty for his actions. Given the situation over, I would send him home this time.

The first task at the training site was hiring a woman to buy our groceries, cook our food, and wash our clothes. The $40 per week was, for us, a bargain and for her an opportunity. For the next six weeks she was one of the highest-paid people in the area. The quarters were good and our 60 students were starting to arrive. Everything looked good. The course, while covering many of the common light infantry subjects, also dealt with recon techniques, concealment procedures, reporting and patrolling. The training area was uniquely suitable and for the training exercise we used the same area as the drug traffickers. While flying around during the FTX, we were amazed at how often we saw coca leaves drying in the open. The excellent fishing here is worth mentioning. A very important thing to remember about the rivers down here: you must be out of the water around 1600. After that the piranha start feeding. We all had fun on this trip.

We weren't alone at the camp. DEA and BORTAC worked out of this location as well. When we got to the camp the first two people I ran into were Donnie and Carlos with the DEA. Their previous years had been spent in 7th SFG, both now having retired from the Army were now working for the other agency. Graduation came with the usual fanfare but was enhanced by the presence of CNN. I would call the student's name and Chief would present his diploma up front. Among our guests were several Bolivian VIPs, including the Minister of Justice.

It was back to Santa Cruz to await the US Air Force but the wait this time wasn't bad. This was industrial fair week and every South American manufacturer was there. Having four to six of the finest-looking Latin American ladies in each booth had a little to do with team attendance three nights in succession. With our funds dangerously depleted, I persuaded the Bolivian Air Force to fly us to Panama if the US Air Force would refuel the plane. The MILGRP commander maneuvered approval through his channels and that was how we got out of country.

December 1993

The rest of the year was a mix of regular SF team training, some three- to four-day trips to Pilot Mountain, and climbing the wall on Pope AFB. We also built a unique climbing wall in the team room. The wall was as tall as the team room ceiling and three feet wide but it leaned back about 5 degrees. The rock on the wall was real though; they had come from the different places we had climbed. John built the wall while I prepared the rocks by grinding one side flat and then drilling a hole. John would then mix JB weld compound to be applied to the back, after which the rock would be secured with a drywall screw. Meanwhile I built a finger board by routing out one-, two-, three- and four- finger holes in a 4 x 6. And last we rigged a 20 foot long overhang route under the loft between the wall lockers.

TEAM LOSSES

Despite the many successes we had this past year, we also had a few losses. Bob Opsitnick became team sergeant of ODA 721. Oscar Santiago was assigned to SWCS. Jauregi, being scuba qualified, was lost to the scuba team. I hated to see Chief Hodge leave, his goals for the team were identical to mine and we worked quite well together.

January 1994

CPT David Tavisolli is our new team leader and with him came the sixth change to our upcoming mission. We're back to Honduras, it would seem. First, though, I'm going to take the team to Camp Dawson, West Virginia.

CAMP DAWSON, WEST VIRGINIA

Wow, talk about cold! We have arrived in the middle of one of the coldest spells this area has had in many years. Daytime temperatures never rose above 10 degrees, and nighttime above -15. We came for training on snowshoes and skis, which I hoped would prepare them for the winter phase of Mountain Warfare school a couple of months away. Despite the arctic temperatures a good time was had by all. We did well on the snowshoes but falling on skis was an art perfected in so many ways. To be fair, though, we were equipped with old-style Army skis, on which no one can do well.

One afternoon we climbed to the top of the mountain. When half of us reached the top, I gave the word to start back down. Down that old logging trail we skied, in the woods with no one to witness our clown like antics. We skied for several days with few mishaps. Lee Metcalf did hurt his knee but it was not debilitating.

HELLO, PANAMA

Our final destination was Honduras but we were made to wait in Panama while the final details were completed. We launched with only 14 hours' notice. Our present mission is to teach a Light Infantry POI again and our waiting time was to be spent preparing lesson outlines and training aids. Little did they realize that we had already done so. Our team was one of the very few with lesson files prepared and training aids at hand. This meant, for us, an 11-day paid vacation in Panama before going to Honduras. During this same time frame had we remained at Ft Bragg we had planned some good Close Air Support (CAS) training with a day on the range with A-10 aircraft. And we could have been home at night with our families. But we were determined to make the best of a bad situation for these 11 days.

February 1994

We're off to Santa Rosa de Copan in Northern Honduras, in the mountains near the Guatemalan border. As with much of Northern Honduras, the area was beautiful, lush, green and so fertile. Many a Virginia farmer would wish for the tobacco fields here. For the historian, there are Mayan ruins and several old towns to be explored. Soldiers from the 12th Battalion would be our students for the next three weeks.

THE CAPTAIN GETS FLATTENED

Another amusing incident occurred as we were setting up at an old monastery on the south side of town. A UH-60 helicopter was delivering a 250-gallon water blivet to our site so the Captain went to the soccer field to guide the chopper in. With the blivet down and cut loose, the chopper was backing up when its prop wash started the blivet rolling down the slight incline of the field. The slope was not steep, but once one of these babies starts to roll, it's almost impossible to stop, like stopping a runaway steamroller.

Perhaps the Captain felt the Honduran soldiers were at risk from the blivet. In any case, he tried to stop it. I was shouting at the Hondurans to stay back when I noticed them pointing behind me. Thinking I was about to be steam rolled, I turned around to see the Captain throwing his body in front of the blivet trying to stop it. He was struck forcibly and bounced, landing on his back. There he lay, spread eagle, dead center in the path of the oncoming blivet. The scene was reminiscent of a Road Runner and Wiley Coyote cartoon, the blivet rolling directly over him. I had thought him dead but he jumped up, seemingly unharmed except for his nose, pushed so far to one side it touched his cheek. With his glasses dangling off of one ear, he assured me that he was OK. Despite his assurance, I sat him down; no way could he be OK after being run over by 2000 pounds.

Chris Patch, our medic, checked him over after which he was evacuated to the hospital at Soto Cano Air Base. He was lucky; three broken bones in his foot and a broken nose were the extent of his injuries. He underwent surgery and casting of his foot. He wanted to return but was ordered back to Fort Bragg as soon as he was fit for travel. Although we wanted him back with us, it was not to be.

So guess who was left in charge of the mission? I appointed SFC Torres as my number two or XO. LTC Butler's confidence in us made us feel good. We were allowed to finish the mission without benefit of an officer in charge. He had not forgotten where he had gotten his training as a young officer, unlike some of his brother officers. The rest of the training progressed without incident. When I visited the 12th Battalion several years later, I saw in their hall of heroes many pictures showing my team members working with the students.

Halfway in the training we took a break. Several of us went to the Mayan ruins at Copan and played the tourist. It was an indescribable site. Because several of us had wanted to visit the site, we spent the entire day there. This summer will commemorate the 100 years since the ruins were discovered, with a new museum opened to display many artifacts.

The mission over, we returned to Soto Cano Air Base and caught a flight home to Fort Bragg, our next departure only seven days after our return.

March 1994

VERMONT

In two rental vans we headed north to Vermont, home of the Winter Mountain Warfare Course at Jericho. Only seven days ago it had been 107 degrees on the runway in Honduras. Now we were in nighttime temperatures as low as -20 degrees. The training covered ice climbing, snow-shoeing, downhill and cross-country skiing, ski-jouring and winter camping/survival skills. Skiing with a 70-pound rucksack on your back is not the way to learn. I would be forever banned from the state of Vermont if they were to discover just who had scarred all those trees that I ran into. But the whole experience was a blast and every man was rated intermediate level skier or better by the end of training.

Our FTX site was Smugglers Notch with seven feet of snow on the ground. From where we got off the buses there was an hour's worth of up hill movement on skis to the campsite. Our tents were erected several feet into the snow; Yukon stoves were installed for warmth at night. From this coziness we went forth each morning to climb the ice and work in the mountains of Vermont.

A SERIOUS CLOSE CALL

I had a near-accident one night in my tent. I awoke from sleep around 0400 hours with an urgent need to urinate. With the outside temperature at -20, I was in no mood get up, get dressed, and go outside to the bathroom. So I persuaded myself that I could wait until daybreak, when we would get up any way. I was soon asleep. Strange as it may sound, I found myself driving down a dirt road, my son beside me. I had that same urgent need to urinate. I stopped the truck, told my son that I would be right back, ran over to a tree and unzipped my jeans to urinate. Just in time I stopped. I was confused; the last thing I recalled was the extreme cold in Vermont. Alarms went off in head. I woke myself up, got out of my sleeping bag, got dressed and ran outside to the latrine. What a close call! I would never have lived that one down. Since that night I have faithfully answered nature's call, if the pressure was sufficient to awaken me. After one more day we broke camp. The bottom of the hill was several miles away and we skied down, laden with 90+ pounds on our backs. No one fell, indicating the great strides we had made since starting.

The following day we felt confident enough to ski at a civilian resort. This was a personal accomplishment. I was elated when I made it down a Black Diamond run without falling or running into the woods. The final of training was spent ski-joring. This is very similar to water skiing, where the skier is tied behind a snow cat or a snow mobile traveling up a mountain or for great distances across flat or rolling terrain. Some of us challenged the driver of the snow cat, daring him to shake us. The four of us flew around the field but hung on for our very lives. Then it happened. It may surprise you to know how far you can soar through the air and land upside down, your head buried in a snow bank. I had to reach in the cavity my body made to retrieve my headgear. But what a ride!

April 1994

April was slow for me. I spent 20 days while on leave on chores around the house. MAJ Orama had urged me to take over operations on the B-Team but I wanted one more year on a team. If he pulled me up there, I told him, I would go find a First Sergeant's job somewhere. I doubt that he found my reply to his liking. But I was reaching that age where it was increasingly more difficult to keep up with the younger men; I wanted one more year before embarking on a different path.

I discussed this with the battalion command sergeant major. CSM Richard Tudor informed me that I was being considered for the SF Group Intelligence Section NCOIC. That wasn't exactly what I wanted either but he said the best he could promise was a six-month delay. There was a first sergeant slot at 96th Civil Affairs Battalion so he recommended I speak with CSM McNamara over there. This way, he said, I could set the date I would go, meaning I could stay on the team for the next few months.

May 1994

I spoke with 1SG Alex Diaz then with CSM McNamara. The job was mine but only after attending the First Sergeant's Academy at Fort Bliss Texas for six weeks. The soonest they can get me in there would be mid July and the course is six weeks long. My time with ODA 722 as team sergeant was near its end. I didn't want to leave yet; there was much more training to be had to bring the team to the level I wanted to take them. They were the best mountain team I'd known in 7th Group but one more year would take them to a level that would set a very high achievement standard. I was very close but I don't suppose it is to be.

SUMMARY

June 1994: This was my last month on the team. Three of the men were attending masonry school at FTCC and SSG Barnard was in sniper school. That would have given us three sniper-qualified team members. In retrospect I was quite pleased with what I'd accomplished with them. When I took over no one had ever been on a rock; now they had made five climbs of 15,000 to 20,000 feet and had evacuated a wounded soldier from 16,000 feet. Eight were lead climber trained and certified. Every man had done ice climbing. Everyone was an intermediate snow skier or better. We had climbed in Vermont, West Virginia, North Carolina, Ecuador and Honduras. Each of our missions went without incident and in excellent fashion. It had been a great experience and worth all the hard work and stress. I will never forget the good times and the guys I had on this team.

Above: SSG Mike Ologue, 721 on the range at Tamara
Honduras.
Below: Old drug lab in the area of Chimore Bolivia.

Above: Coca leaves dry in the yard at a remote location in the area of Chimore Bolivia
Below: SFC Bob Torres brings a litter with a man in it down the face of a clift during training in Veermont.

Above: Our 117 man class in formation on day 1 at Santa Rosa de Copan, Honduras

Bottom: Students fire on the range we built at Santa Rosa de Copan, Honduras.

Students rappel down under the watchful eye of SFC Torres.

Below: Students use a rope suspension bridge to move across the gorge 70 feet below.

Above: Another photo of students using a rope suspension bridge to move across the gorge 70 feet below.

Below: Students of the 12th Battalion receive instruction on map reading. That's me standing

Above: SFC Bob Torres flags a CH-47 in as SFC John Barnard hooks up the water trailer.
Below: I stand beside figurine at the Copan Ruins.

Above: SFC John Barnard dressed for the weather.
Below: SSG Mike (Doc) Halterman takes a break to admire the view several hundred feet above a pass in Vermont.

Above: I shot this photo while in Vermont looking back down the mountain at the other climbers on the rope behind me.

Above: The statue at the gate of the Ecuadorian 9th Battalion in Latacunga Ecuador.
Below: The mountain Cotapoxi in the distance.

Above: The view from 15,000 feet up on Cotipoxi.
Below: LTG Timmens and I chat at 14,000 feet.

Above: My partner in the street dance.
Below: SFC Barnard and an Ecuadorian soldier STABO away dangling 100 feet below a Puma helicopter.

Two shots taken while on a team climb at Pilot Mountain, North Carolina.

July 1994

I'm heading for the First Sergeant course at Fort Bliss, Texas. I was appointed as the First Sergeant of Company A, 96th Civil Affairs Battalion before I left. I drove to Texas so I could take my climbing gear because I planned to climb on Waco Tanks on the weekends. I also planned to visit some friends along the way. In Dallas I spent the night and visited a military museum on the east side. I visited with Jan and Margaret Coates, Don Carr and Bob Pinkston showed up as well and we all went to dinner.

THERE'S AN ACCIDENT BEHIND YOU

Back on the road I continued to Midland, Texas, and stopped at the Confederate Air Force hanger to look at vintage aircraft for two hours. I drove west and had gone only a few miles out of town when an east bound trucker on the CB said there was one hell of a wreck behind me. In my review mirror I saw a Chevy rolling end over end, raising a dust cloud. I wanted to keep driving but couldn't so I pulled over to the left, crossed the divider and headed back. It was a gruesome sight, with wreckage strewn about. Twenty-five feet away, on the service road, lay the man who had been ejected from the rolling vehicle. I checked him first. He appeared to have sustained a fractured leg and skull but was still breathing.

Then I noticed smoke billowing from the wreckage. If there were a fire there, the driver would need help so I ran to the vehicle. Inside was a large, very pregnant woman. The left side of her scalp was peeled back but she had a pulse and respiration. Her

183

door was jammed so I dashed to the passenger door. By this time others were stopping. Help was enlisted from two truck drivers who I asked to extinguish the fire while I continued with my own efforts at freeing the pregnant woman. I crawled inside and cut the seatbelt to release her but she was too large to maneuver. And the fire was scary. I didn't want to be inside if the vehicle blew but I didn't want to leave the woman.

A power company vehicle pulled up just then and the men came over. They had a bar which we used to pry the door. Several of us tried anyway but the door refused to budge. So I used the bar to pop the hood so they could put out the fire. Meanwhile I had the power company truck reposition. We wrapped a chain through the door window frame then the truck was driven forward. I hammered at the door latch with the bar until at last it gave way and the door swung open. It was during this a carload of emergency room nurses stopped to help. The smallest of the group crawled into the wreckage to treat the woman while the others treated the husband. God must have sent these guardian angels; they were simply fantastic. I directed some men to keep the crowd back because many were in the way. The fire truck finally arrived but by that time the fire had been extinguished. The firemen continued to move the crowd back. They spread something on the leaking fuel and made sure the fire was out. Next the ambulance arrived. The pregnant woman was laid on a backboard. This was after the braces on the back of the seat had been cut so her leg could be freed up.

It was late and the excitement had died down. I was tired, dirty and thirsty so I drove back to Midland and stayed the night. When I thought back on what I had been part of, I was heartened by the efforts of so many to save the two people on their way back to California from a high school reunion. I was interested in the outcome. When I called two weeks later the two were still in the hospital.

AT LAST, FORT BLISS

I reported to Fort Bliss the day before the course was to begin. The course was somewhat disappointing and not what I had expected. It was mostly busy work and lacking in structure. I had attended better.

The welcome weekends were spent climbing Waco Tanks, about 25 miles north of El Paso. Most often I would do some boldering but a few times I met experienced climbers who allowed me to climb clean-up with them. The clean-up man climbs last, removing from the cracks the protection pieces that had been installed to prevent the lead climber from dropping too far.

August 1994

After graduation on August 23rd I eagerly left for home; I had missed the family. At Fort Ben Harrison I dropped off some paperwork then continued homeward. I anticipated spending some time with the family before my next deployment. I began to suspect this was not to be. While 16 hours from home, I called and Josie gave me the message from the company to report immediately upon my arrival. But after making a few phone calls I felt the situation was not that critical, so I went on to the house. I was sure glad to get home.

September 1994

DEPLOYMENT TO CUBA

Within two weeks I was packing for Cuba from where preparations were being made for the US invasion of Haiti. We would deploy to Cuba, which was to be the staging area for Special Forces, Rangers, PSYOP and Civil Affairs Forces from USASOC. I was Senior NCO for Civil Affairs (CA) assigned to Joint Special Operations Task Force (JSOTF Raliegh) headquarters. As often happened, it was during the weekend that we were alerted the mission was a go. The Major and I were first to get word so we were the first at the company, calling our people in. I had just hung up the phone when the Major strode in, fuming. He said, "First Sergeant, you won't believe what Mrs. (so and so) just did. I called there to tell her husband to come in. She cussed me out and told me her husband wasn't in the Army on the weekends. She had stuff for him to do so I was not to call their house on the weekend ever again. Then she slammed the phone down! What do we do now?"

"Watch this," I said to him. I picked up the phone and called the Sheriff's office. A deputy was soon dispatched to the house to have the husband report in. After a 10-minute interval, the phone rang. It was the wife, demanding to know if I had sent the deputy to her house. Yes, indeed, I snapped at the woman. I told her not to say a word until I had finished. I told her the fact that her husband lived at home was a privilege, not a right. If she ever again cussed at the MAJ, me, or anyone from the company who called on official business, or left any doubt that her husband would get the message, her husband would be moved into the barracks. She and the kids could visit him in the evenings and weekends! Is that understood, I asked. Having established her clear understanding, I hung up before she could reply. In the doorway the Major was laughing and no longer angry.

Thanks to the Air Force, the trip to Cuba took several days. We departed Fort Bragg on a C-5. When word was given that we were 45 minutes from Cuba and I grabbed one last catnap. I awoke as we were landing, not in Cuba but in Dover, Delaware. An AC problem had apparently developed, making it necessary to turn back. After repairs another attempt would be made in the morning. With this in mind, we left everything on board to get food and sleep. To COL Boyatt, 3rd SFG Commander, I volunteered to remain aboard so everyone could leave their weapons. A couple of others also volunteered.

About 0400 we were awakened by noises below. The Air Force was loading our equipment in another plane because this one could not be repaired. I went back to sleep after explaining that we would move the personal stuff and individual weapons when the others returned later that morning. Not 30 minutes later two airmen came upstairs and started grabbing weapons and equipment to move to the other bird. On looking up they were greeted by the unwelcome sight of my 9-mm pointed at them. I ordered them to put everything back down on the seats, to get back down the ladder and to tell whoever had instructed them to move the stuff to forget it—we weren't moving it. We were relieved around 0600 so we could eat. When everyone had returned, we moved everything to the other aircraft. It was probably around 0900 when we took off again, not too far because this plane also developed problems and had to turn around. We wondered if the invasion would take place without us. That afternoon the Air Force informed us that we could not take off until the following morning because the crew needed to rest. They had been up too long and couldn't fly until morning. As they had done little since our return, I was skeptical. The third time, however, was a charm and we got to Cuba at last.

I STEAL THE INTERPRETERS

18 Sep 94: I stood with the company commander, MAJ Mike Czaja (Chii) by our tent on the hill next to the airbase and watched as an Army truck discharged more soldiers. I noticed something different about those soldiers and told the Major so. "Right, from 40 yards away you can tell that there is something different about those guys. First Sergeant, you've been in the sun to long!" was his cynical comment. I decided to speak to them, betting on their being French and Haitian Creole speakers. He wondered how I could tell. I pointed out the way they

stood, all wore either an Army or Marine uniform, they were thin and all were black.

As I approached, I made note of their names: all were French. It turned out they had been sent from different posts or forts to Fort Bragg and from there boarded another airplane to fly here. Additionally they had no idea where or to whom they were to report. I introduced myself, telling them they would be working for Civil Affairs. They were to follow me and I would get them assigned to a tent. They would be provided a cot and equipment. I was leading them our tents when the Major approached us. Was I helping them, he asked. Sir, I replied, I am taking care of our newly arrived Haitian speakers. I said, if you can't talk, you can't do the mission. They now belong to us. While our new members were setting up in their tents, I took a roster of my new interpreters to Task Force J-1. I informed the J-1 if others arrived, they were to be directed to me. That same story was repeated to J-3, who asked if theirs would be assigned. I told him one would be assigned to each of my tactical support teams (TST) and one TST to each of his companies. That left two, one for me and one to lend as needed to various elements of the Task Force. I then assured him of my assistance and support.

Heck that worked so well that once in Haiti I told the TF Mountain G-1 the very same story. By the time I left Haiti, I had amassed about 30 interpreters. The entire time there my deception had gone undiscovered. Just before I was to leave I asked the 3rd SFG commander, COL Boyett to take good care of them. Was I giving up command and control to 3rd Group he inquired? When he discovered what I had done, we both laughed. He'd have done the same thing, he told me. I had assigned the men judiciously and fairly, ensuring their availability where most needed. The commander agreed, reporting no complaints from his staff about our support. Thinking back on it, the intended assignment might have been to his unit anyway.

THE INVASION IS CANCELED

Invasion was imminent. The MH-53s were loaded with soldiers, rotors turning, momentum building for take-off. It was an awesome sight and sound. Escort helicopter gunships, Cobras and Apaches, were also powering up. All this activity must surely have been detected by Castro; this end of the island was rumbling and shaking. Then the unbelievable happened! The order was given to shut down—there would be no invasion. We were instead to go in as peacekeepers where just minutes before we had been aggressively preparing for the 90-mile, one-hour ride to wage battle. We were angry in our disappointment, having spent days planning and preparing, and getting psyched up. At the same time, however, we were relieved.

What the future held for me personally was not known at this time. But within the next few days I would be asked to do conduct a mission, the magnitude of which would cause my name to be written in the USASOC historical write-up. The mission was nothing I would have suggested but it would be mine, nevertheless, directly from BG Richard (Dick) Potter. How we went into country was changed. To quote John Wayne, "Go to Plan B." What this meant no one knew, but Special Forces and Civil Affairs excel in going with the flow, meanwhile developing the plan, which is exactly what we did.

September 1994

GENERAL POTTER FINDS ME

My second night in Haiti I went to the command tent, where everyone seemed edgy. It was because General Potter was in the J-3. Everyone jumped to attention as he exited; everyone, that is, but me. MAJ Cazja was elbowing me, saying he was coming. I continued to work, my cap pulled further down on my forehead. As the General strode by I pushed my cap back and cleared my throat. "How are you, sir" I greeted him. He said he was fine and turned to look at me. He recognized me, stopped and reached out to me as I stood. We shook hands and slapped each other on the back while many bodies collided behind him. It was great to see him again and he seemed to feel the same. He wanted to know what I was doing there and I informed him I was working for him again as the Senior CA NCO on the ground and member of the JSOTF. Great, he said, assuring me that he would have to find something special for us to do. Had I only known!

I knew BG Potter well enough to understand the impact of his words: enjoy the calm now because the storm is coming. COL Jim Powers best described GEN Potter as the type who, upon entering a task force headquarters and finding 100 people of all ranks standing idly, would search for the first man wearing a Special Forces tab. Rank meant little, E5 or O5. He would approach this man, tell the man he was Special Forces and command him to take charge. The man was to kick butt, get things organized, and to tell anyone who questioned him that "he said to do it that way." He would then say that he would be back in four hours, expecting things to be running and a briefing to be ready. His belief that the Special Forces soldier would get things done never wavered. I held him in such high regard that I felt his retirement was a real loss to the special operations community.

True to his word, he got me the next night. We were in his nightly staff meeting when he ask "where is 1SG Johnson"? I called out from the back of the room and started moving forward, He told me to get on up there so he didn't have to break his neck trying to turn around. Once up front he told me he had a mission for me. He then said that Major General Mead, General Shelton and he, had determined a mission just right for me, or so he said. He was silent a moment and I thought, well here we go! He then outlined what was to be the mission of my life. "First Sergeant, we want you to turn the electricity back on in this country. That means everything outside of Port au Prince and Cap Haitian is yours." The place was deathly quiet while everyone, including me, let this bit of news soak in. I wondered how the hell I could pull this one off? The how of it he would leave to me but priority was to be given to those towns where there were Special Forces.

SPECIAL NOTE: The following pages are from the draft notes by Dr Fischer, USASOC Chief Historian at the time. He was responsible for writing the official Special Operations historical summary, which was later classified because of material in the first two chapters. There were changes made to the unclassified draft given to me by Dr. Fischer before it went to final copy and there is nothing classified in the following. The parenthetical comments are mine.

START

Expectations regarding the repair of infrastructure created the need for an expanded role for Civil Affairs soldiers while at the same time serious questions remained about how to pay for projects. Lacking any other alternative, Civil Affairs soldiers took many matters into their own hands. A wider involvement of Civil Affairs soldiers became possible when the JCS authorized a more permissive approach to the expenditure of funds for civil affairs projects. A Joint Staff Message on 20 Oct 94 authorized commanders to expend DOD appropriations to accomplish those projects considered essential to the performance of the MNF mission (such as projects of a temporary or emergency nature) and delegated determination authority for each specific mission to the on-scene commander.[91]

With authority to widen their mission responsibilities, Civil Affairs soldiers developed a

---

[91] Joint Staff Message, DTG 2013311Z Oct 94, to CINCUSACOM.

number of innovative projects to facilitate the functioning of the Aristide government. These projects were kept limited in number and specifically focused on key aspects of the infrastructure.

Undoubtedly the most far reaching civil affairs project to take shape was Operation LIGHT SWITCH, a campaign to restore limited electrical power to major urban centers outside Port-au-Prince. Some areas had been without electricity for nearly three years. The idea for restoring electrical power originated with BG Potter. He saw the effort as critical to restoring a secure and stable environment while improving the security posture of the JSOTF personnel scattered throughout Haiti. On 26 Sep 94 BG Potter delegated responsibility for the organization and the execution of the project to 1st Sergeant Ronald Johnson of Company A, 96th Civil Affairs Battalion. Johnson remembered thinking, "How the hell am I going to pull this off"[92] To Potter he simply promised that he would begin working on it immediately. Potter made it clear that he expected staff officers to assist to the fullest extent possible.

(I jokingly told GEN Potter, the JSOTF Commander, Sir, if you don't mind I'm going to leave your staff meeting now and get started on this unless you have something else for me?

---

[92] Misc notes of 1SG Ronald Johnson, 96th CA Bn, located in USASOC Archives, Ft Bragg, NC, 7.

He replied, no that's OK, I think this will keep you busy for a couple of days.

From the staff meeting I headed directly to the Intelligence people and requested all available information on power plants in country. While that was being collected, I went to the CMOC and briefed LTC Powers on my new mission. En route back to the office, I detoured to 20th Engineer Brigade to look for power engineers. Here I struck gold; there were two from Army Prime Power. Their OIC, CWO Hanchet, agreed to help in any way they could. Two NCOs were duly assigned to assist me.

MAJ Czaja was in the office. He had become dispirited and discouraged by the seeming impossibility of this mission. He offered his help, though. I asked him to keep the jackals off my back and the curious out of my way, and to handle most of the briefings. In the end I would make him look good.

I had to see some of the plants myself to determine requirements so I asked the JSOTF Deputy Commander for a chopper. The General was going out in the morning so he checked to see if my two men from Prime Power and I could hitch a ride. Approval was granted. The next morning we flew into Jacmel with the General. We were still evaluating when the General was ready to leave. I told SSG Sutton to stay with the ODA and SSG Zyzyk and I flew to Les Cayes. Back at PAP 30 or more reporters awaited us. The General's security team got off first and we jumped off with them.

The General offered the use of his chopper for as long as I needed it to retrieve my other man. Unknown to me, my son was at a friend's house that evening when all this was televised. The friend's mother recognized me and called him into the living room, where he saw me on the news. He watched as the General and I talked and then saw me and SSG Zyzyk board the helicopter. This meant a great deal to me, his seeing me doing something very important.)

Johnson quickly set to work organizing the effort. The initial stages went well. Transportation and parts were two issues that required immediate attention. For the most part, these assets fell quickly into place. The first real problem was a legal one, namely, how the project could be funded. At first

Potter assumed that Title X monies could be used under the guise that the lighting project was necessary for the safety and security of US soldiers. Regulations stated that Title X funds could be used for such projects if they were "dominimus" in nature defined as being within the scope of what a squad of soldiers working a day to accomplish at no more than $1000 in cost. The scope of the project easily exceeded these constraints. The JAG section of the JSOTF quickly recognized the problem and attempted to rectify the situation by requesting that Department of State approve the project. A request for approval was sent through channels to ACOM. In less than six hours ACOM approved the request with JCS and Department of State concurrence soon to follow. The letter of the regulations was ignored under the mistaken assumption that the project could be kept limited in scope and duration.[93]

(Actually, I suspected we were headed for trouble and asked JAG to check it out. A draft message had to be approved by the General and sent ASAP. I remember being awakened at 0400 hours with the message that the mission was a GO. Everyone was amazed by the speed with which a mission of this magnitude had been approved; it was unheard of.)

---

[93] CPT James Patterson, 16 Dec 94. Interview conducted by Major Joseph R. Fischer, USASOC History and Archives.

In less than four days time, Johnson orchestrated the necessary coordination with 3rd SOSC, 10th Mountain Division DISCOM, 18th Airborne CORPS COSCOM, TF Mountain J-3, the CMOC, 10th Mountain Division Aviation, 3rd Special Forces Group, 20th Engineer Brigade, Army Prime Power and the Army Boat Units out of 7th Transportation Battalion. He secured commitments for fuel, batteries, and oil. Along with the commitments came four 5,000 gallon tankers, four 2,500 gallon HEMMIT tankers, two contact maintenance trucks with two men each, four 500 gallon blivets with a CH-47 helicopter to move them around the country. The Army Boat Unit made available three 2000 class LCUs and their dive team when and where required.

The project began on 28 September 94 and was linked to a psychological operations campaign to prepare the countryside for Aristide's return. 1SG Johnson along with members of the Army Prime Power unit conducted assessments of electrical generators at several sites. They were under no illusions as to the difficulty of the undertaking. Many of the generators were inoperable due to inadequate maintenance, lack of spare parts, and contaminated fuel.[94] These problems had their origins in the ineptitude of the Cedras government, the impact of the embargo, and the antiquated condition of much of the equipment, some of which dated from the U.S. Marine Corp's previous occupation of the country. The fact

---

[94] Fuel contamination is common in diesel fuel that has sat for extended periods. Bacteria contamination is the most frequent culprit.

that many electrical workers had not been paid for months further complicated matters.

(The day before the mission began we had a final coordination meeting in the General's tent. He was to have been out all morning but returned unexpectedly. I quickly explained why we were in his tent. He said great, spoke briefly, then left, asking to be notified when we were finished. Apparently he had not been told we planned to use the tent.)

Potter wanted to know how soon Johnson could have fuel out to at least to a few Haitian cities and Johnson promised that it would be done within seventy-two hours of the assessments. Johnson kept his word. On 30 September, Johnson assisted by SFC Jeffery Curtis, of A/96th, headed off with a convoy consisting of two HUMVEEs, two 2500 gallon HEMMITS, a 5 thousand gallon tanker and two contact maintenance trucks departed the Light Industrial Complex in PAP and headed down the road toward the cities of Jacmel and Petiet Goave. Twenty-five miles west of PAP Johnson leading the 5K tanker, turned south toward Jacmel while Curtis led the rest of the vehicles down the road to Petiet Goave.

The road to Jacmel traverses difficult terrain as it crosses the volcanic mountain range separating PAP from the villages along the southern coast. In places the incline of the road is very steep and long with a number of switchbacks making the drive hazardous.

As the two vehicle convoy was climbing the last mountain before the descent into Jacmel, the heavily loaded 5K tanker reached a point where it would go no farther up under it's own power. The road was just too steep. Rather than wait for a recovery vehicle to happen by, Johnson attempted a field expedient solution to the problem of getting the under powered vehicle over the mountain.

He backed his HUMVEE up to the front of the tanker and fastened a tow chain to the tanker. The HUMVEE provided just enough power to allow the tanker to slowly proceed over the mountain.

(The tow chain was made from the four cargo ratchet straps I had in the back of my HUMVEE. The look from the tanker driver told me he thought I was out of my mind. I instructed him to engage the front wheel drive and wait for my hand signal. I placed the HUMVEE in low range 4-wheel drive and 1st gear. Once ready I raised my hand and motioned to start forward.

When the front of the tanker lifted upward, I gave the HUMVEE the gas; surprisingly it started forward. I could even shift into 2nd gear as I pulled the tanker uphill. A Major, who was coming down the mountain, stopped and got out of his vehicle, motioning me to stop. I ignored his request and nearly ran him down; he bolted away. His mouth agape, he stared in consternation at the sight of the 5,000 gallons or 40,000 pounds of fuel that I was pulling up the mountain.

Later that night the General asked what I'd have done had my vehicle not been able to pull the tanker. I replied that I would have hooked the Major's to mine, and that failing, I would have stopped the first civilian truck driving buy. As a last resort, I'd have flagged down an oncoming bus and had the passengers push by hand, if that was what it took. Because I wasn't going to stop that close to town)

When the small convoy arrived in Jacmel, it received a warm reception from the townspeople who had not enjoyed the benefits of electricity for nearly a year. Cheering crowds lined the streets as the American vehicles drove through town toward the power plant. After stopping at the power company office and the police station, Johnson delivered his cargo. It was not long before the generators were up and running again. There was insufficient fuel to provide twenty-four hour electricity. All that could be promised with the initial delivery was that there would be enough fuel available to run the generators for four hours every night. For the residents of Jacmel four hours was enough. For several days after Jacmel's generators were back in operation, the arrival of night and the first flickers of electric bulbs coming to life were cause for celebration.[95]

(A week after the power plant at Jacmel had been started up, I was at JSOTF HQ planning another run when the BG Potter and COL Boyatt came in. Johnson, it was your fault, they declared. Their accusation surprised me; I could think of nothing I'd done that was blameworthy. The harangue continued until finally one of them said, "Let me tell you what happened. We were in Jacmel this evening when one hell of a commotion started up. It sounded like an attack was building, with all the shouting and cheering. We grabbed our weapons and moved to cover. The SF team laughed at our reaction. We told them we were concerned about what was going on close by! Still laughing, they said the celebration signaled the coming of the electricity for the evening. With that both of them laughed.)

After the initial convoy, Johnson and his men worked the undertaking into a routine. They delivered

---

[95] Misc notes of 1SG Johnson

fuel, oil, and batteries. Soldiers from the Army Prime Power detachment provided technical support. The Americans and their supplies arrived by land, sea or air depending on the situation and location. At Ansed D'Hainhault, where the power plant had been inoperable for nearly three years, the celebration started before Johnson and his crew could get into dock when a boat loaded with 25-30 Haitians came out several hundred yards and started singing to them. Once the delivery team arrived at the dock a city-wide celebration broke out. It took the Americans over an hour to move a mile from the dock to the power plant because the streets were crowded with people celebrating the expected return of electric power.

(Ansed D' Hainhault was also scary for us, the first time we went in, for several reasons. No other American was in the town. There were only the three of us senior NCOs with a dozen young soldiers. At the dock where we first landed, we first heard of the very dangerous Haitian colonel in town and of murders he had committed or had his men perform. In his office the colonel tried to grill me about my security measures. Looking into his hate-filled eyes I realized that he was very dangerous. I instructed my interpreter to give the colonel a literal translation of my words using my exact tone and not to leave any cuss words out. I advised the colonel not to concern himself about my *!# security. There was a Special Forces scuba team on one boat, with mortars and at least four 50-caliber machine guns; plus there were more than enough soldiers on the two boats. As an added measure I told him there was a Ranger company with helicopters within striking distance just hoping for a fight. My security was not his #!* concern but rather ensuring that none of his men caused any problems for my men was. While I hadn't come there to arrest anyone, I would if circumstances dictated my doing so. The young interpreter was shocked at my forceful tone but managed to do as I said. My threats weren't outright lies but the colonel couldn't be sure. He did, however, have his men remove their side arms and leave their other weapons at headquarters. When I visited Jerime two weeks later, I saw him looking through the bars of a jail cell there.)

It was the same story in Jerime. Johnson and his team had finished their work and departed the town by LCU. Darkness had fallen over the city. With the boat several miles off shore, the lights began appearing in homes and along the streets as section after section of the towns electrical grid was energized. On the LCU, the soldiers stopped what they were doing and gathered to watch the lights. In the distant city, the night had fallen back a little and the sounds of cheering people could be heard over the sounds of the sea.[96] Progress comes in small steps in Haiti. Over the next twelve days, Johnson and his teams delivered fuel to seventeen cities and towns across Haiti.[97] As of 6 December 94 Civil Affairs personnel had supervised the delivery of nearly 130,000 gallons of fuel.[98]

From a psychological operations perspective, LIGHT SWITCH provided a clear message to the Haitian people that conditions were improving. The fact that the improvement was linked to the efforts of American soldiers also proved a benefit and immeasurably assisted the working relationship of 3rd SFG(A) soldiers working with the Haitian people.[99]

---

[96] Ibid., 30.

[97] The following cities received fuel under the Operation LIGHT SWITCH: Jacmel, Petite Goave, Gonaives, St. Marc, Jeremie, Ansed D'Hainault, Les Cayes, Hinche, Port de Paix, Ft. Liberte, Ouananminthe, Belladere, Aquin, and Thiote.

[98] MEMORANDUM for Commander, JSOTF, Subject: Top Ten Civil Affairs Projects prepared by MAJ Steven G. Meddaugh, 6 Dec 94, 1.

[99] 1SG Johnson ran Operation LIGHT SWITCH with a skeleton crew of key people for an undertaking of such magnitude. In addition to Johnson a number of other soldiers were key players in making LIGHT SWITCH a success: SSG John Sutton and SSG Thomas Zyzyk of Army Prime Power, CPTs Thomas Kelly and David Oskey of 10th DISCOM, SFC James Dale Hartman of Service Company, 3rd SFG(A) and his number two NCO SFC Jeffery Curtis of 96th Civil Affairs.

The program did point up problems with the ability of the Aristide government to function, however. LIGHT SWITCH was always intended as a short term project that would be quickly turned over to the Haitian government. It was an Army project ran by an Army 1SG and a small handful of soldiers. Despite the Clinton administration providing over $200 million of assistance to the Aristide government soon after its arrival for the purpose of getting basic services functioning again, the new government showed little inclination to assume responsibility for LIGHT SWITCH and was more than willing to allow the Americans to keep Haiti's lights glowing. Deadline after deadline for the end of the U.S. Army's involvement in LIGHT SWITCH came and went as the inertia of the Aristide government threatened the nation with a return to darkness should the deadline be kept. As early as 16 October, LIGHT SWITCH was due for termination in ninety-six hours and COL Boyatt had given instructions to find someone to "torque up" inside the Aristide government to get electrical workers paid so that the generators continued to operate when the Americans stepped away from the project.[100] The ninety-six hour limit passed without workers being paid or the government taking any steps to assume responsibility for the project. Several weeks later, ACOM requested that JCS cancel the program because of the funding issue and ordered Civil Affairs personnel to stop all deliveries. At the time the message went out to the JSOTF, one LCU filled with

[100] Miscellaneous notes of Major Joseph R. Fischer dated 16 October 94.

fuel was already enroute to Anse D'Hainault. Before the ship could off load, the crew was ordered to turn around and return to Port-Au-Prince.

The psychological cost involved with once again casting the nation back into darkness proved more than the JCS was willing to accept. Soon after the request to stop LIGHT SWITCH arrived, the JCS rejected it and ordered ACOM to resume fuel shipments. The following day, the LCU began its return trip to Ansed D'Hainhault.

LIGHT SWITCH remained an ongoing operation for the U.S. Army well into January 1995. With the draw down of Army logistics assets, SOF planners had hoped to turn over responsibility for fuel deliveries to Brown and Root, a U.S. company who had assumed responsibility for logistical support to Operation UPHOLD DEMOCRACY.

THE END OF THE OFFICIAL HISTORICAL DRAFT WRITE UP

I will now continue with the rest of the story, the part omitted from the official write-up.

OTHER ACCOMPLISHMENTS

Many more actual events were left unmentioned in the official write up. Quite often, after the power plant was running, I would dispatch someone to the phone companies for those generators to be activated. Enough fuel was given with which to charge their batteries, enabling them to stay open 12 hours a day. The townspeople were thankful for the chance to communicate with family members who lived elsewhere. Hospitals in surrounding areas were similarly dealt with. One of us would check the generator there and would leave enough fuel for its use in times of emergency when the power plant was nonfunctioning. In our few hours in town we worked feverishly to get done as much as possible.

BG POTTER GETS SERIOUS

On the eve of our first run into Jacmel there were still no tasking letters from CMOC to the TF Mountain J-3 authorizing support by their units. That the letters were needed had been known for 48 hours but not one had been received. At 2100 hours I went to the CMOC to check on the letters. The Colonel in charge was hostile and angry. Shaking his finger in my face, he informed me spitefully that he didn't work for me and furthermore didn't think the operation was necessary. The letters would be available when he felt like doing them. What was there for me to do but salute and reply "Yes, sir!" With difficulty I removed myself from his wrath and headed back to the JSOTF and BG Potter.

I appraised BG Potter of the problem—why, where and who. His response was grabbing my arm and hauling me with him back up the street. En route I told the general that despite LTC Powers' insistence that the letters be written, the CMOC Director failed to do anything. On entering the office the general pitched his cap onto the colonel's desk. That action was executed to perfection. The cap landed on the desk, rotated, then came to rest, with the star directed at the colonel's face. BG Potter then casually introduced himself and directed everyone to sit. This conversion would be limited, one way as we call it. The general talks and they listen! At the conclusion, he turned to me. "First Sergeant, they will do what you need, how you need it and when you need it, or I will send someone home with something they don't want." He walked about ten feet then turned around. "Powers, we haven't talked in a while. Come take a walk with me." That left me and the colonel eyeing each other warily. He then asked me what I wanted. I replied, "Sir, you know what I need. I'll return in an hour for it. Thank you." With that I left, hoping that I never had to work for him.

SLEEPING IN STRANGE PLACES

I worked until around 0400 hours in the morning the day we were to make the first run by sea and was therefore thoroughly exhausted and bone weary. But I had to be at the dock by 0700 hours. If I went to my sleeping area, there was the chance I would not awaken in time. I had an inspiration. The General's command tent was empty. Someone on the night shift could awaken me there. Stretched out in the general's chair and covered up, I was soon fast asleep in the air-conditioned tent. At 0615 someone was shaking my arm and waking me up. My eyes focused on BG Potter. He asked me what I was doing and I hastily explained that I had worked late and was concerned that I wouldn't be awakened in time if I slept down in the warehouse. I figured if the person who was to awaken me from the J-3 nightshift forgot to do so, the general would because he was an early riser. He told me to go back to sleep but I told him I needed to be on my way, thanked him for the use of his chair and left.

AN ONBOARD SEAFEST

When we left Ansed D'Hainault the first time, one of the locals asked how he could thank us. I thought a moment then asked where I could buy some lobsters, about 30 of them. He rushed off and returned 20 minutes later with the 30 lobsters. He would take nothing for them but I insisted. We agreed on $20. The cook on the LCU was forbidden to prepare anything that had not been inspected by a food inspector. I cooked the lobsters while she cooked shrimp, french fries, hush puppies and cole slaw. The entire crew, the boat's and mine, all feasted on this bountiful meal.

AN EMERGENCY ON SHORE?

We arrived offshore at Port de Paix at 2200 hours, our second trip to the town. Two miles offshore we dropped anchor and settled for the night. I was in the mess hall playing cards when a SP4 rushed in exclaiming, "First Sergeant, the Skipper wants you on the bridge. There's something going on ashore!" Up on the bridge the captain related having seen a flare fired from shore and someone flashing lights trying to signal us. I observed the lights for a moment and asked the skipper if he had a Morse key for his light mounted on top the bridge. While they looked for it I stepped outside and on a lark took my mini-mag flashlight and signaled to shore with Morse code "Slow down." I twice sent di, di, dah to see if they would acknowledge and "stand by". About then the skipper called out they had found the Morse key and were hooking it up. Meanwhile while they were doing that I scribbled a message, translated it into Morse code, and broke it down to five-letter groups. I was never a commo man but when I was younger everyone on the team had to learn to send code. The old saying was everyone should learn to ask for help and if someone sent something back you could at least fool yourself to the end thinking help was on the way.

When I began to send to those guys with that Morse key the world lit up. The light on top the boat was probably a couple million candlepower or more. I told them there was no 18E on board but if they had an FM radio, to go to a particular frequency. They acknowledged and in short order we were talking. Their wish was simple: a real meal aboard the boat tomorrow morning. We all had a good laugh about it. The skipper agreed and I told them what time we would be ashore.

At breakfast the next morning they told us how the Haitian colonel had become scared at the signaling with lights. With the big light they were even more shocked. This was because I started with the small light and suddenly there was a light burst from hell. The Haitians wondered if we were going to invade their town and wanted to know why.

FOOD FOR LABOR

That day in Port de Paix an unforeseen problem came up. Evidently the plant manager, who had not been paid for several months refused to work any longer because he could not even buy food for his family. After a moment's thought, I asked the CA officer and team leader to get the mayor. When the mayor arrived, I asked if he could persuade the local merchants to donate enough food every week to feed the plant manager, his two workers and their families. In exchange the plant would continue to operate daily. Before he left to negotiate, he was told that unless there was agreement from all concerned, I could not unload the fuel. He hurried away but returned shortly with news that the local merchants had agreed. All that was needed now was for the men at the plant to agree, which they did after some persuasion. We then unloaded and got on our way.

THE FIRST HAITIAN LCU DIVING CHAMPIONSHIP

After one of the fuel runs I decided to reward the young soldiers with a much-needed break. They had worked diligently and had had some frightening moments without any accident or incident. I asked the skipper about dropping anchor and letting them swim in the calm sea on this beautiful day. His men had been asking the same thing. We moved to a site where the water was 85 feet deep and so clear that patches of grass on the bottom could be seen. My team assembled on deck in PT uniforms or swimsuits. The weak swimmers were issued life jackets and buddy teamed. I gave a safety brief then the skipper lowered the ramp and everyone got in the water, including a girl who had never before gone swimming in her life. She was scared to death but I had one arm and another soldier had the other. Once in the water she soon relaxed and grew confident in the life jacket. Several of the others stayed close to her and to the weak swimmers. I appointed myself lifeguard until I felt everyone would be okay.

The boat crew had built a diving board off one side of the bow. I was invited to join them. I feigned reluctance while egging them into competition. They agreed, not knowing that I had been a diver in my younger days. Each man dove, executing his best dive; they were quite good, too. At last it was my turn. I eased onto on the board, testing it for spring, as I went. They thought I was nervous when I got to the end and turned around. They encouraged me just to jump and I would be okay. I sprang backwards off the board and executed a one-and-a-half with a half twist and dove in. When I surfaced the skipper was ribbing his guys about how an old 1SG had suckered them in. He declared me the winner.

I also dove from the bridge of the boat, a distance of 45 or 50 feet. A little while later a crewman suggested a swim to shore. I was game for that but first had to get a hat to prevent further sunburn on the top of my head. After doing this, I went to the bridge, where the skipper informed me that it was 3400 meters to shore. I had to think seriously about this. I had done a couple of 5000 meter swims in the remote past and had not done one farther than 2500 meters without fins. Feeling bold and daring, I threw my cap off the bridge, climbed up on the handrail, dove off, retrieved my cap, and started swimming. Every 20 or 30 minutes one of the young soldiers would go to the bridge and ask Skip if I was okay. He would find me with his binoculars and see I was still swimming. I was smoked when I reached shore and did not relish the idea of swimming back. The skipper wisely sent the work boat after us and towed us back to the boat. Along the way we passed over a bed of star fish. Without needing to voice our thoughts, each of us released the towline and dove for the fish. The depth was deceptive and quite a long way down. I snagged one, turned and kicked off the bottom heading for the surface. The work boat turned around and picked us up again; this time we went on to the LCU. I had planned to bring the star fish home but unfortunately left it on the tail of the boat.

DO YOU KNOW MY BROTHER?

We were in Petite Goave topping off their fuel tank at the plant one morning when a Haitian lady asked if I could help her find her brother. At first I thought he was just one of many Haitians who, before our arrival, thought they would be arrested by the police and simply disappeared. It was not our job to look for missing persons but I would take his name and turn it over to someone who could perhaps help. She then said her brother was in the American Army and was here in Haiti. I was caught me off-guard but recovered and asked for his unit. She didn't know that but she did know that he was in the Army and was here in Haiti. I asked where he was stationed in the US. Again she replied that she didn't know but he was in the American Army and was in Haiti. What did he do in the Army? Again the same reply. I was frustrated, believing there was no way I could help her. Then came the clincher: she had never met him. I explained to her that because of the size of the American Army, it would be almost impossible for me to locate him. By now she was frustrated. In desperation I asked for his name, which I planned to run through the Task Force Mountain J1 when I got back to PAP. I would not be overly concerned if nothing came of it. She stated his name was David Cadet; I asked her to repeat the name. David Cadet she exclaimed.

Shaking my head in disbelief, I grinned at one of the men, who grinned back. I then told her that her brother was not in the Army but in the Marine Corps, that he was in Haiti and that he worked for me. What a stroke of luck, given the odds. I promised he would visit her soon and asked for her name and address. I also took a photograph of her with the Polaroid. She further explained that he was actually her half-brother whom their father had taken to the States before they ever knew of one another or met.

Back at PAP I had CPL Cadet report to me. I questioned him about his activities in his spare time. He assured me he had done nothing wrong. I then informed him that a young woman had come to me that day in another town. She knew plenty about him and had been searching eagerly for him. He was very worried now. I continued, telling him of my concern because this woman had some very interesting things to say, compelling me to investigate further. He persisted in his innocence. I then showed him the picture, adding that perhaps it would help him remember. I covered with my thumb the note she had written. He was looking intensely at the photo when I dropped the bomb. She said she was your sister, I told him, and removed my thumb.

His eyes widened and he exclaimed, "1SG, this is the sister I have never met. I only learned of her a year ago from my father." The rest of the men, who were privy to the ruse, had a good laugh. We were all happy to bring him the unexpected good news. I promised him sufficient time to visit his sister in the next few days. With that I went to dinner at the mess area.

In the mess area BG Potter beckoned me to his table. He questioned me on the day's events. Those I narrated to him, saving for last the story about Lance Corporal Cadet. He thought it was great. I shared with him my idea of making the reunion a PSYOP affair. He agreed and added his own thoughts. His chopper was mine to use, if necessary, to bring it about.

Spotting Cadet in the chow line, I asked the General if he wanted to meet the man himself; he was eager to do so. I then had Cadet report to the General. Given the fact that in the Marine Corps generals do not speak to corporals, Cadet was understandably nervous. When General Potter placed his arm around Cadet's shoulder to assure him he would meet his sister, Cadet appeared ready to pass out. When he was finally dismissed his gait was uncertain and he was sweating profusely. The reunion between brother and sister took place much sooner than anticipated, throwing our plans in disarray. But we managed to arrange a small area for the meeting, with cake and Kool-Aid on a picnic table at the PAP Industrial Complex. Here he met his nephew and nieces while the PAO photographed the event. The article even appeared in the Marine magazine.

ONE MORE TIME

After four days of planning and twelve more busily running all over the place, there were sixteen plants running on a limited basis. A second run had been conducted to top off the tanks in those locations. Our replacements had been in country for more than one week and the three other members of my company were now back at Fort Bragg. I was scheduled to depart the next morning; the orders were in my pocket. I now had people working in four countries. In Panama they had a full load with 5000 Cuban refugees. My last task was to visit and thank those who had supported the operation. I was walking past Task Force Mountain when I heard the general calling. I turned around as he came quickly and threw his arm around my shoulder. He said, "1SG, we just got word, we're going to make one more run."

I made no mention of the orders in my pocket. I returned immediately to TF Headquarters to begin the process of restarting the program that night. After three days, the last run was completed to all the sites. This was possible because I had known the exact fuel capacity for storage tanks. Again I said my good-byes, this time fully intending to leave. I ran into COL Haluskie, who informed me that the General had insisted I attend one last staff meeting that night. I thought perhaps he wanted a briefing on the final operation and perhaps what would be needed should another operation be deemed necessary.

A SPECIAL AWARD

The intended purpose of the staff meeting that night was still unclear to me. The meeting differed from the usual in that that only the J2, 3, and 5 would brief that night; when J5 finished, we were all to stay because the General had planned something special. I expected him to thank everyone for a job well done and to introduce his replacement to JSOTF, Admiral Richardson. It made perfect sense to me; he was due to leave in two more days.

After the J5 briefing, Admiral Richardson walked to the front. Potter directed me to come up front too, where CSM O'Donahugh handed the admiral a small package. By this time I was thoroughly confused. From the package Admiral Richardson pulled out a picture frame with a one-of-a-kind certificate naming me "Honorary Senior Chief Master Sergeant." Potter announced to everyone that COL Boyatt, CSM O'Donahugh, the Admiral and he had this certificate made up in appreciation for the extraordinary accomplishments I had made during Operation LIGHT SWITCH. Both Potter and O'Donahugh had signed it. The Admiral presented the certificate to me, after which he pinned the Navy rank of Senior Chief on my pocket. To be honored this way by Potter and Richardson, who together had probably 55 years working Special Operations, was very significant to me. Potter had been with Delta at the onset and in Desert One. He served with SF in Vietnam and other theaters. Admiral Richardson was the first naval flag officer to come from an exclusively Special Operations background. This included the Navy equivalent of Delta.

BG Potter joked with the Admiral that his 1SG had more sea time in this operation than he did and wanted to know why. The Admiral asked him acerbically why, if he liked the 1SG so much, did he make me do one final "Light Switch" run when there were departure orders in my pocket. The General was puzzled and asked what he meant. Pointing to me, the Admiral encouraged Potter to ask me himself. Potter eyed me critically as I retrieved the orders from my cargo/leg pocket. Why didn't I say something, he asked me.

Unhesitatingly I said, "Sir, I knew this was your last mission in the Army. You leave here in two days and retire on the 8th of Nov. I figured that if I could stay here a few more days and make sure that you could get out of here with everything running smoothly, what the heck! Besides the orders are good for another 24 hours and I'm scheduled to get on a bird in the morning." I could see his eyes glisten with unshed tears. Our mutual respect was made manifest by our actions, something that occurs seldom between two soldiers with such a disparity in rank. When he retired on November 8th SF lost a heck of a leader.

AWARDS SIGNED AND DELIVERED

I could not leave the country without ensuring that the numerous people who had supported our mission would receive something as well. By 0230 hours that early morning I had completed all the awards and letters of appreciation. I went to the general's tent hoping to find him. He and COL Boyatt were both there and signed some 34 letters of appreciation and 10 awards. Afterward I set about delivering these. Two captains were roused out of bed around 0400 in the morning by a runner who awakened them with the news that Operation Light Switch was on again. They were visibly surprised to find me in the S3 shop to present them with ARCOMS. No one had ever heard of a 1SG running around in the middle of the night presenting awards and letters of appreciation. When all was said and done, I boarded the plane heading for Ft. Bragg.

WHY ME FOR THE MISSION

Immediately before leaving I said good-bye to the General. I asked him why I had been picked for the mission since I had the lowest rank in the room.

There had been more than 40 there, at least 10 of whom were LTCs or COLs. Why me? "I've known you for a long time and I wanted to get it done quickly," he said, adding, "I knew you could get it done and I knew most of those in there couldn't." I thanked him, saluted and left.

A SPECIAL THANKS TO THOSE WHO HELPED

I doubt another mission of such magnitude will ever be given me, and with such unequaled support. For my accomplishment I was submitted for an ARCOM. However, MG Meade of the 10th Mountain Division and Commander of Task Force Mountain upgraded the award to an MSM. That remains my proudest and most memorable accomplishment. There were many soldiers who worked diligently to make it happen. Each admitted to a feeling of pride and satisfaction when we went into yet another town where townspeople would cheer our coming and thank us for our help. This was the best they had felt about themselves and their mission. Several times one or more had shed tears of pride and joy. They were very proud to be an American in the Army.

HONDURAS

8 Nov 94 and I'm heading south with my soon-to-be company commander, Del Clark. Our first stop will be in Honduras at JTF-Bravo to check out our J-5 office there. My company maintains an office there year-round. Our men are sent there usually for 90 to 120 days each time. But the current op tempo means six months or more will be spent here before the men

can return home. From this location we are the theater commanders lead for all civil military operations in Central America. While in Honduras we will inspect a number of projects that had been coordinated by our people and some that are due their inspection 18 months after completion to ensure they are being used as intended.

We arrived at Tegucigulpa, (Tegu) a little after lunch, rented a vehicle and drove to Soto Cano AFB about an hour northwest of the capital city. In Soto Cano we linked up with our men in the J5 shop, MAJ Jerry Thomas, MSG Alex Diaz, SFC Greg Vanyur, Harold Velez and Dennis Bell. They updated us on where the others were and what was going on. The main information we sought was which projects were scheduled for Honduras, El Salvador and Guatemala. I found time to visit an old friend, LTC Angalica, whom I had known when I worked at the Special Warfare Center in the mid-eighties.

The next morning we left out early to go visit some of the sites in the northern part of the country. The first two sites were in the vicinity of the town of Santa Rosa de Copan. The schools looked great. The construction crew had also built a really nice play ground area with swings, sea saw, basketball court and so on. The teacher was really proud of her new school. We stayed in town that night and I went up the street to the 12th Battalion Headquarters and saw some of my friends up there. It was nice to see them again. It was strange at night though because this part of the country was on a electricity rationing program and shortly after dark the lights went out. Unless you were where they had a small generator that meant you were in the dark. It made the walk back to the hotel very interesting.

The next morning we left early for Tegu to review a couple more sites en route. That night was quiet and the following morning we boarded the plane for Panama to check on our men working in the Cuban refugee camps in Panama. We would also attend the Overseas Coordinating Conference (OCC). This conference was held twice a year and is where we would determine which missions we could fully or partially support in the upcoming 12 months.

PANAMA

Our men were performing quite well under some very trying conditions. Two men worked in each of the four camps, each of which had about 500 people. The Cuban occupants even elected a mayor as their representative. Our men established schools with playgrounds, and churches as well. This last was very significant since Cuba at the time discouraged religious worship. We were well aware that Castro had sent some of his military and intelligence personnel with the refugees to cause trouble at some point. There were already rumors of riots planned for a later date.

They did, in late November and into December. During these riots our men did some really remarkable feats. In an early incident about 30 MPs were preparing to storm a mess hall in which 25 Cubans were holed up. SFC Tony Guerro walked up to the scene and asked what was going on. The lieutenant told him but after learning which ones were inside Tony said their planned action wasn't necessary; he would talk to the Cubans. The lieutenant tried to stop Tony, who simply walked to the chow hall and told the Cubans he wanted to come in and talk. He was allowed inside and within 10-15 minutes had persuaded the men inside to come out.

During an earlier riot SFC Jackie Wilson had dashed back inside the camp and through a mob to rescue a fallen U.S. Military Policeman inside. He had to knock down a couple of the Cubans but he was quite large, weighing more than 200 pounds. Green, a young sergeant from the company, was also well liked by the Cubans, although that was not the reason he had no trouble in his camp. Like Wilson, Green was not only huge but had also played linebacker at Alabama until a knee injury. He had reportedly told the three biggest Cubans in his camp that although he really liked them, should there be trouble in his camp, he would kick someone's butt and he intended to start with them. On hearing this the J5, LTC Maggie Risher told Green he couldn't say such things. Green apologized to her but refused to recant because he would lose face. His point was difficult to argue since his was the only camp that did not riot.

The rest of our week was spent at the Hotel Panama in the OCC conference. Afterward we were able to visit the camps a few more times before we left the country. We were to be involved in operations throughout Central and South America next year, building about 30 schools, drilling 50 or more water wells, building a half-dozen clinics and conducting disaster training. It would be an interesting year.

AN OLD FRIEND SHOWS UP

While at the OCC I ran into LTC Gil Perez, my old company commander during Operation JUST CAUSE in Panama. He was now deputy MILGRP commander in Ecuador. It was good to see him again.

YEAR'S END 1994

I'll probably be home for Christmas this year and I think that's great. Since 1989 in Panama Christmas has meant a lot more to me; my family has yet to understand why. As for my company, I wish I could bring all the men home for Christmas but unfortunately sometimes it's not possible.

FINAL COMMENT

That's it, five years in the life of a senior NCO in Special Forces. My story is free of killing, maiming, sex and similar things that might appeal to a wider market. I did so because I wanted to include readers of all ages.

If you haven't figured it out by now, we in Special Forces are just like anyone else but we are willing to find ways to overcome challenges that may discourage others. We make our share of mistakes but like to think we recover more quickly from them and move forward. We are nomads who take an interest in the communities in which we live. And yes, some of us are adrenaline junkies who do not want the mundane. But know what? We enjoy life because we understand above all else that life is short and life is valuable. Someone once said that you are never more alive than when you're close to death or accomplishing the impossible. De Oppreso Libre.

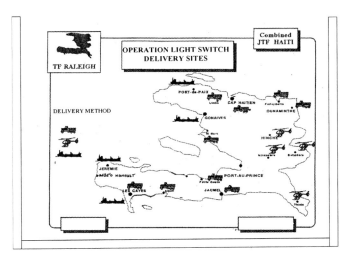

Above: A map of Haiti showing how each site was to be supplied fuel for power.
Below: One of the 2000 class LCU's of 7th Trans working for us with our equipment loaded.

Above: I confer with Civil Affairs personnel on a second LCU while at sea.
Below: Me with some of the young troops that worked for me.

Above: SFC Hartman and I walk down the street in Ansed'd Hanault leading our vehicles while locals celebrate our arrival to turn the electricity on
Below: Translater relates to the Colonel what I just said. Over the colonels right shoulder stands an individual that towns people told us had killed a number of people and was feared by them.

Above: Majors Del Clark and Jerry Thomas speak with the teacher a site near santa Rosa de Copan, Honduras where a new school had been built the year before.
Below: Inspection of one of the many water wells drilled by U.S. Army Engineers in the area of La Union, El Salvador

Above: Myself and MAJ Steve Foster my last commander in 96th Civil Affairs.

Below: A U.S. officer inspects a power plant we restarted. In the forground a V-16 diesel powering an electrical generator.

U.S. and Honduran soldiers along with civilians work together to build new schools. The kids really enjoyed helping finish their school in this manner and it gave them the opportunity to get to know Americans.

Above: We practice a message pick up technique.
Below: Take-off for a parachute jump with jumpers sitting in the door.

Above: Jumper prepares to land moments later.

Above: The author near a mountain top in Trujillo, Honduras in April 2002.

Printed in the United States
87680LV00001B/118-150/A